D0641654

Inspired by
Listening

This book is dedicated to my parents, without whom this book would not be possible. Throughout the years, they have been a constant support, always encouraging their daughter to accomplish her goals and follow her dreams.

Thanks for everything!

Inspired by Listening

by
Elizabeth M. Peterson

Yeogirl Press
Hampton Falls, New Hampshire

an imprint of
Yeoman Press

2006

Copyright © 2006 by Elizabeth M. Peterson

All rights reserved.

The purchase of this book entitles the buyer to reproduce student pages for classroom use only, not for commercial resale. Reproduction of these materials for an entire school or district is prohibited. No part of this book may be reproduced (except as noted above) without the prior written permission of the author, except by a reviewer, who may quote brief passages in a review.

ISBN 0-9638595-5-2

Cover design by: CRAFTMASTERS® – Sikeston, MO USA

For information, address:
Yeogirl Press
PO Box 303
Hampton Falls, NH 03844
musicbiz9@repusa.com

1 3 5 7 9 10 8 6 4 2

Contents

All listings written in *italics* are reproducibles you may copy for your students to use.

Part Three
Background Knowledge

Introduction

Inspiring our Students

We provide inspiration for our students everyday: a poem, a personal story, a famous quote, artwork. Music is also something that inspires students. They may enjoy playing it, composing it or performing it, but don't forget listening to it. Listening to music is the most basic of all ways to appreciate music and yet it is often overlooked as a means from which students become inspired to learn. Whether you are a music teacher or not, listening to music can be part of your teaching repertoire. You can use listening experiences to teach, reinforce and enhance the curriculum you currently teach.

Is This Book For Me?

This book is for ALL TEACHERS who have a love or appreciation for music and would like to share that with their students. You do NOT need to be a musician to use this book. You DO need to be a teacher who encourages your students to explore music, welcomes their love of music in the classroom and is willing to give them musical opportunities to learn. The strategies found in this book are adaptable to all age groups and abilities.

For Music Teachers!

As a music teacher, you will be able to use this book as a comprehensive unit of study where students learn the value of listening to music. This book will show you how to introduce the art of listening to your students as you learn strategies to encourage your students to listen actively. The activities and lessons will give them opportunities to respond to, interpret and speak intelligently about music. Everything from introductory lessons about listening to a meaningful assessment is included in this book for you.

For Classroom Teachers!

As a classroom teacher, you will appreciate the practical applications this book has to your teaching situation. You will be able to integrate many of these active listening activities and lessons in a meaningful way that connects to your core curriculum. You can collaborate with your music teacher or do this on your own. Either way, your students will appreciate the innovative opportunities you will provide for them.

How Do I Use This Book?

This book is separated into three parts:
1. Teacher Overview – This section gives you the basic knowledge you need to know about the three types of listening as well as a guide for how to use the active listening experiences in your classroom.
2. Lessons – This large section takes you through all the steps to implement active listening activities and lessons into your classroom.
3. Background Knowledge – This section provides all kinds of information on composers, musical genres and helpful references. It also contains two complete projects that deal with background knowledge you can use in your classroom.

Whether you are a music teacher or general classroom teacher, you will find this book to be a great resource. You can use the activities and lessons to implement a complete unit or pick and choose what you would like to use for a one-time project.

Why Active Listening?

Years ago, when I began to take over my cooperating teacher's fifth grade classroom during my student teaching, she encouraged me to do something with music, since she knew how much a part of my life it was. That weekend, I thought and thought about what I could do. The school had just been visited by Dennis Kobray, an actor-musician who does a phenomenal presentation of composer Ludwig van Beethoven's life and works (as well as other musicians), so I knew that his presentation was still fresh in the students' memories. I knew I had to pick something fairly short to keep the students' interest as well as something familiar, if possible. Beethoven's beautiful piano piece *Für Elise* seemed to be an obvious choice and the students already knew the basic story behind it from Kobray's presentation. I thought we could interpret it by scribbling and by a brainstorm of words. As I thought of more ideas, I got excited. We could write a letter using our brainstorms to write the words that Beethoven couldn't find! On Monday, I started the group of lessons with my students. By the end of this project, the students had a great understanding of who Beethoven was, what the rondo form was, and were able to use their letter writing skills to interpret the music. The students were proud to share their letters and Mrs. Emily Morency, the teacher, was thrilled with this integrated work.

During the rest of my student teaching, Mrs. Morency, who noticed the students' new motivation to write, encouraged me to continue this integration of music. So, I arranged for there to be time for students to listen to music during their language arts class and with that, new interpretation lessons were developed. The Khatchaturian cartoons, the Vivaldi violin monologues and the rhythm settings were three more that were created. Besides that, I began to develop my beliefs and my theory of integrating music into the classroom. "Active listening," as I began to call it, was becoming a real teaching tool that could be used and the outcomes were very rewarding. Students grew to love music as they listened to it actively and they were using their language skills to respond to it in various ways.

The next fall, I started my first job as a second grade teacher at the Centerville School in Beverly, Massachusetts. While there, I arranged for there to be active listening time every day for my students. During snack time, my second graders listened to everything from Mozart to Duke Ellington. I took them on a musical journey through time, concentrating on a composer or musician each month, listening to their music, one piece a week. Sometimes we danced to it, sometimes we drew what we imagined, sometimes we talked about it and sometimes we wrote about it; but we always enjoyed it: listening together and sharing in the experiences. Not only were the students enjoying the music in the classroom, but their parents were as well. Many parents commented throughout the year on how much they appreciated the focus I put on music in the classroom.

About two months into that school year, I was fortunate enough to enroll into a Master's program at nearby Endicott College. I found out about it one day and started my first class the next. It was a degree program in Arts and Learning and it sounded like the perfect program for me. During my time there, I was able to develop more lesson plans for my repertoire and received much encouragement and applause from my peers and professors.

Since some undergraduate classes at Gordon College, my arts-based research class at Endicott gave me another chance to see what others were doing in the field of listening. I was pleased to see that my basic ideas were supported in the literature I read, even literature that cited examples from the 1930s. One person's writing in particular caught my attention. It was that of modern composer William Schuman who had written an introduction to Aaron Copland's *What to Listen for in Music* (1939) in 1988. Many of his views on listening to music supported mine. He especially concentrated on the importance of listening to music actively.

> "The first prerequisite for listening to music is so obvious that it almost seems ludicrous to mention, yet it is often the single element that is absent: to pay attention and to give the music your concentrated effort as an active listener."
>
> –William Schuman

Obviously the idea of listening to music is not new. It is, of course, the most natural thing to do with it. However this approach of making it a part of the general classroom routine by encouraging students to listen actively and integrating those experiences directly with the curriculum seemed relatively new.

Now, as a music teacher, I have applied the same ideas to my lessons with a new perspective. (Sometimes my students wonder why the language arts are integrated into their music class so much.) It is only by becoming active listeners that they can truly become lifelong learners and appreciators of all kinds of music.

Acknowledgments

Years have passed since I first started typing out my ideas on my once-new laptop. My biggest supporters have been my family. It is through my dad Richard Trask's gift of writing and my mom Ethel's gift of publishing, I have been able to create this book. There have been many drafts and many late nights. It would have been impossible to complete this without them. My husband Brad's patience and encouragement is endless. Even my infant son Zachary has been supportive in these last weeks allowing his mom to have good nights' sleep and productive days at the computer putting on the finishing touches. And I would be remiss not to mention my little "sesame seed" who will meet the world soon!

To Dr. Bruce Gleason – A great music professor who encouraged my integrated approach to teaching and showed me the value of the writing process.
To Emily Morency – My cooperating teacher who allowed this once sprouting novice to try out her new ideas.
To Stephanie Grenadier – A caring teacher and friend who challenged me to see things in a new perspective in order to constantly develop my thoughts.
To Roger Craft – A friend who has provided me with valuable, professional opportunities. His support and encouragement are greatly appreciated.
And to the nameless interviewer from the Portsmouth, NH, School System who, when seeing my portfolio of student work in active listening, said I should publish my ideas – Thanks!

I am fortunate and excited to share these ideas with you! If music interests you, I guarantee that this will be appealing no matter what grade or subject you teach.

PART ONE

TEACHER OVERVIEW

The Art of Listening

There are many ways in which one can listen to music. Just think about some people you know and you may find that each one listens to music differently. There's the young child who dances to music played at an outside concert in the park, the couple who eats a candlelit dinner to classical music, the teenage boy who blares music through his speakers in his room, the young girl who cries at the sound of a love song, the old man who closes his eyes to listen as he sits in the front row at Tanglewood, the person who listens to the radio in the car ... the list could go on and on. Think of when and how you listen to music. Is it when you are alone with a CD player or while you are doing chores around the house? All these styles of listening are very different but have a place in the *listening spectrum* found on the following page. This spectrum can be divided into three main styles of listening: passive, responsive, and active.

The passive listener is one who allows music to be in the background, where music takes second stage. Have you ever sat down to read a book for pleasure or as an assignment and your mind wandered to other things: the conversation next to you, a list of things you need to get done, your growling stomach, things you'd rather be doing or to a faraway island? When you get back to the book, you find you're on the next page – but you haven't absorbed a word you just "read." You have blocked out the meaning behind the words. That's exactly what happens when you have music on and you're doing homework, reading, or talking with a friend. Your mind, in an effort to accomplish two different goals, is switching from one thing to the other and not gaining any true value from either one.

The responsive listener is one who is engulfed by the sounds of music. The music tends to drown out other things around him and becomes the main focus. Often the music is loud, creating an atmosphere of pure sound in an attempt to encapsulate the moment.

To the responsive listener, music is a means to heighten emotion. He may use it to get energized or relax. A heavy rhythmic piece can give a sense of power or drive to accomplish difficult tasks; while Pachelbel's soothing *Canon in D* relaxes the mind at the end of a hectic day. Often, young girls in love will listen to countless hours of "sad" music in order to heal a broken heart. (I know I have.) Some young boys love to listen to music very loudly through surround-sound speakers which allow them not only to hear the music but also to feel the vibrations of it, creating a multi-sensory experience. And how many times have we seen one of our own students walking around with ear buds stuck in their ears? There are many young adults who love to be surrounded by music. In these ways the listener wants the music to control the body in some way, taking it to new dimensions.

The active listener concentrates on the music itself and thinks about it. He uses his intellect and emotion at the same time to hear what is happening in a piece of music and respond to it.

The Listening Spectrum

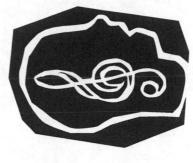

	Passive	Responsive	Active
Traits	• music is in the *background* • person is doing something else while music is on • person doesn't respond to music much, if at all	• music is used to create an *atmosphere* • music is often loud • person responds to overall mood of the piece with heightened emotion	• music is the focus • person *thinks* about, questions, and deciphers details of a piece • person interacts with the music intelligently as well as emotionally
examples	Listening • while eating dinner • while reading a book • while doing homework • while thinking about other things • while chatting with a friend in the car	Listening • to fast music before a big game • to relaxing music on the couch after work • to music during a long car drive to stay awake • while dancing or singing	Listening • and deciphering the meaning of the piece through the lyrics or other musical elements • and drawing an illustration that comes to mind from the music • and paying attention to how the melody, rhythm, harmony, etc., move within the piece • while recognizing old motifs and finding new surprises in the music

These three categories may seem very concrete. Listening, however, is not always this black and white; there are, as with most things, gray areas. For example, sometimes listeners will fluctuate between passive and responsive listening or between passive and active listening. The categories have been made so that you may better understand how listening can be different from person to person and from place to place. Creating a place that fosters active listening will be the main goal of this program.

For most, it is hard to listen actively all the time. Being able to recognize how you and others listen will be important. This chart will help you. Your students will also benefit from understanding how to differentiate among the different kinds of listening habits. Using some of the activities found in Part 2 of this book, "Getting Your Students Ready to Listen," (page 25) to introduce these ways to listen will be very helpful in getting the most out of the active listening experiences.

Active Listening Process

The process for conducting an active listening experience is very similar to that of a reading program. In a reading program there are things done before, during and after reading. The same applies to listening to music. Before you listen, you must know some *background* about the genre, composer or piece. While you listen, you are concentrating on the *experience*. You are becoming familiar with the music by listening to it many times. After you listen, you *interpret* what you have just experienced by making judgments about the music.

Knowing the *background* of the music we listen to can be beneficial. We can learn about the composer, the time in which he/she lived or the style of the piece. Before we begin a new story we may read the short biography of the author, look at the covers and the pictures or think about the setting of the book and the characters using the given summary.

As soon as we begin to read a story we are *experiencing* it. As we read or hear Cinderella for the first, fifth, or twentieth time, we remember things, get more details of the story, and anticipate what is coming. Sometimes experience can go deeper when we relate to the story in some personal way. If you ever had a domineering, judgmental stepmother, you are sharing a deeper experience with Cinderella as you read the story. You understand her emotions. The same goes for listening to music. The more we listen to a piece of music the more we experience it. We remember main themes, hear the detailed layers of the instruments, anticipate familiar or favorite parts and even pick up on new surprises.

After we have experienced a piece we are open to *analysis* and *interpretation*. We think about and discuss what the piece means to us, making judgments about it, the instruments and even the composer. When we analyze or interpret a story we are discussing it, writing about it, and making judgments about it, the characters and even the author. While analysis and interpretation usually come after the experience, as we become better readers and listeners, we often are able to interpret as we experience.

Active Listening Process

Before . . .

Background Knowledge

Understand the basic background of a genre, composer or piece of music.

During...

Experience

Familiarize yourself with the music through repetitive listenings and guidance from the teacher.

After...

Interpretation

Use the skills you have already been taught and the skills you are learning in class to analyze the music and express your interpretations of your listening experiences.

Overview of Active Listening Experiences

An active listening experience should be purposeful and meaningful to both you and your students. To ensure that this happens, here are some key points to consider.

PICKING OUT MUSIC

You should use a great variety of music from all sorts of genres. This will help keep the interests of a variety of students. Don't be afraid to play popular music as well as classical music, program music and opera. If presented in a positive atmosphere, the kids will respond positively. A list of suggested pieces and the types of recordings to have available in your classroom can be found on page 166.

For a class of beginning listeners, the music must be relatively short since the students may not be used to listening to long pieces of music. As the time progresses, so will each student's attention span and interest in listening, allowing for longer pieces. You are, in a sense, building their listening stamina.

When picking out music, don't limit yourself to recorded music. Think also about **live performances**. There may be a student who is willing to play her latest recital piece for the class, invite a teacher or other staff member to play, a parent volunteer may be looking for just this type of opportunity to visit your class or play for your students yourself. Live performances, especially done by those your students know, are much more exciting than recorded music. The only thing to consider if you do this is that having a one-time performance will not provide for repetitive listenings, which are so important to active listening. Here are a couple of ideas of how you can make live performance work with active listening experiences:

- Have a recording of the same piece available to listen to later when you need to listen again.
- Record the person who is performing (with their permission, of course) so that you can play the performance over again when you need it. Use audio or video for this purpose.
- If the performer is available to you on various occasions (For example, if you or one of your students is the performer) have that person play the piece when needed.

ACTIVE LISTENING STANCE

During the time students are listening to music, they should be in an "active listening stance." This could be anything from sitting up straight to putting one's head down on the desk. Maybe you want to allow students to find a special place in the room. Of course, as teacher, you do need to be aware of the occasional student who sees this as certified sleep time. You set the parameters. The stance is a preparation to actively listen to the music about to be played. It should be a comfortable position where the listener can enjoy the music.

SETTING ASIDE TIME

If you are a classroom teacher who wants to use active listening experiences, you will need to set aside about 10-15 minutes every day through the duration of the project to listen. This may seem like a burden, but there is a way to make it successful and if done well, this can be very beneficial for all involved. This time could be at the beginning of the day, during snack, after lunch or recess or at the end of the day.

When I did this in my elementary classroom, we listened during snack time everyday, all year long, focusing on one composer or genre a month. Sometimes we would integrate the experiences into other parts of the curriculum, other times we just listened as a class for the pure enjoyment. No matter what we did, we would listen to one or two pieces of music for a whole week so that we could get the most out of our listening experiences.

As a music teacher, time needs to be allotted at the beginning of a class or at various times throughout a class, depending on the lesson. The same applies for a teacher whose time is limited to a class period.

LISTENING FOR THE FIRST TIME
The first time students listen to a piece, they should do it for pure enjoyment and be allowed to give their first impressions about the music. This can be done orally through discussions, on paper in sentences (journal) to be kept and referred to later, or any other way you may think is appropriate.

LISTENING AGAIN
After students have had a chance to hear the music once, they will need to hear it again and again. This is a very important step and can easily be overlooked. However, in order to really understand what's happening in the music, the listener needs to take the time and listen more than once.

Each time your students hear the music, they will pick up on new things in it whether that be details in a story they see in their imaginations or details in the music itself. You can help them along by encouraging discussions by *setting purposes,* asking *guided questions*, and conducting *active listening activities*. Ideas for how to guide this type of instruction can be found in Part 2, "The Active Listening Experience," on page 40.

FIRST FULL LISTENING EXPERIENCE
Your students should get an opportunity to try out active listening in a simple manner, before they are expected to use musical terms or literary devices as a means to analyze or interpret what they hear. For their first couple of times, they can listen to and explain what types of things they get out of the music, like what images come to mind. Once they have done something like this, they will be more motivated to continue actively listening to other music. A detailed lesson that does this can be found starting on page 47.

SETTING AN EXAMPLE
You are modeling for the students that listening to music is important. It is often said that during "Sustained Silent Reading Time" teachers should also be reading to show that reading is important to them. So is the same for listening. Listen to the music with your students. It is a great experience that should be shared.

Modeling Good Active Listening Skills

As with anything else, a good teacher will find opportunities to model the behavior they are trying to teach. Listening is no exception. Good listening habits aren't just about making sure you aren't doing things while the music plays; it goes further than that. As the teacher, you also need to model how good listeners *think* when they listen actively.

THINKING OUT LOUD

How to do it:

1. Play a short excerpt of a piece of music and have the appearance (exaggerate, if necessary) of listening intently to the music.
2. Stop the music and then think out loud by saying what is going through your mind as you listen.
    - "The dynamics here are really loud, that's *forte*. And it sounds like the main instruments here are trumpets, but I can also hear those big drums. What are they called? Oh, ya, timpani, or kettle drums."
    - "This song really reminds me of fireworks on the fourth of July. I can see all the different colors bursting in the sky."
3. Continue the music and play another short excerpt.
4. Stop the music again and think out loud.

Helpful Hints:

- You may want to do this for an entire piece of music (2 minutes should be your maximum for this activity) or for a section of a larger piece.
- Have in mind the types of things you want to say when you stop the music. Doing this ahead of time will help you focus in on what types of things you will want your students to listen for as they begin to actively listen.
- Your students should be observing you only and not intervening … yet. After you have had the chance to model this type of active listening behavior a couple of times, pick another piece of music and invite students to interject their ideas when the music stops.
- This modeling can be used when introducing one of the active listening activities too. For example, model "words and phrases" by playing an excerpt, stopping it and writing down words/phrases that come to mind. These activities can be found on page 43.
- DON'T FORGET! Sometimes people do listen passively or responsively and it is all right to model that too. If you play a song that just makes you want to dance, explain this to your students and then get up and dance!

Collaboration and Integration

What is Integration of Music?

Collaborating with other teachers can be rewarding and often fun. With this program, the integration of music is different than the traditional norm. Here, the collaborating teachers are focusing on both the music and the curriculum; both have equal importance. When this happens, two things occur: the students are learning about the music as they experience, analyze and interpret it and other parts of the curriculum are being taught, developed or reinforced.

During music class, students are developing their music skills and during other classes they are using the listening experiences as mini field trips to interpret the music. For example, after actively listening to and studying some program music in music class, students will write a narrative in language arts using the music as a springboard for inspiration. Instead of using music to interpret the curriculum, you use the curriculum to interpret the music.

Using music to interpret the curriculum:

Examples:
- Learning songs to memorize math facts, historical dates, the presidents of the United States, etc.
- Learning a song with dance movements that help students to understand and remember the life cycle of the butterfly.

Using the curriculum to analyze and interpret music:

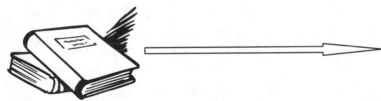 

Examples:
- Listening to a piece of program music and writing a story to it.
- Writing down nouns, verbs, adjectives, and/or adverbs that go with a piece of music and defending why you chose those words in a paragraph.
- Comparing two pieces of music in a Venn Diagram or other graphic organizer.
- Writing a music review that uses music vocabulary to describe a piece.

Many teachers allow music into their classrooms in the manner of the first example. While they are using music, they are not taking full advantage of the students' ability to use music and think critically. Being able to collaborate with other teachers while teaching your students active listening skills is a way to integrate different curriculums in a meaningful and thoughtful way. The music is first experienced, then interpreted using other parts of the curriculum.

There are many benefits to collaborating and integrating your curricula with that of other teachers. Here are a couple of them:

- It helps get or keep other teachers involved with what students are doing in music class.
- It is great for sharing common experiences (listening experiences) and helps build community within a class.
- This may be just what you are looking for in terms of a fresh new way to go about teaching things you have been teaching for years.

Integration Ideas

Active Listening Time in the Classroom

If you are a general classroom teacher who knows the value of music in the classroom, you may want to have active listening time during the day in your classroom. If you teach in an elementary school, this may be an attractive idea. Sometimes in middle school, times can be allotted when the team has "team time" or if the team can schedule some time into their day. This may be difficult to implement in the high school grades, but not impossible. The first couple of minutes of a language arts class can be devoted to active listening and reflection in a journal where students can later pull ideas for future stories, poems, etc.

When I taught in a second grade classroom, my students listened to music everyday during snack time. Later, I would use these listening experiences to enhance other parts of the curriculum. Maybe you want to do the same.

If you are a music teacher, you could be the one to introduce the musical concepts as well as the music itself and the classroom teacher could follow up and allow time for repetitive listenings. Allowing for this time is important to keep students interested and listening. Students need repetition in order to fully experience a piece of music. More information on this will be presented in Part 2, "The Active Listening Experience," beginning on page 40.

Share Lesson Plans

Regardless of where and when the active listening time takes place, the classroom teacher can take those experiences and integrate them with his or her current curriculum. Many of the activities and detailed lessons that are outlined in Part 2 of this book take listening experiences to the next level: interpretation. Interpretation can be something you do in music class but also in other classes as well, especially in language arts. There are many ways to integrate the language arts into the interpretation of music: poetry writing, story writing, letter writing, development of the parts of speech, etc. Share the lessons from this book with each other as well as the format of the lessons (page 45) so that they can be adapted to different genres of music as well as different age groups.

Put a Music Center in Your Classroom

A music center is a great place where students can explore music on their own. This is something that nearly any teacher can do without becoming overwhelmed. There are many things that can be put into a music center, for example:

Books and articles about musicians and music
Tape and/or CD player with headphones
Instruments
Pictures of musicians and instruments
Staff paper and pencils
Small keyboard with headphones
Small Instruments
Small radio

Collaborate with Teachers of All Subjects

Don't limit yourself to collaboration and integration between music and the core subjects only. Collaborate with the computer teacher by having students develop Power Point presentations that define music vocabulary words or the life and times of composers you study. Have students use Publisher to design and publish the "Make a Performance Program" assessment described at the end of Part 2 starting on page 112. Collaborate with the librarian to arrange time for students to research some of the composers and musical genres you listen to in class. Collaborate with the art teacher by integrating the different time periods of history as seen through art and architecture. The physical education teacher may want to collaborate by teaching students different dances that also accompany these time periods. Actively listen to the music that the PE teacher uses during these classes. The possibilities are endless!

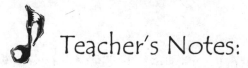 Teacher's Notes:

PART TWO

LESSONS

Example Lesson Timelines

The following two timelines are examples of how active listening experiences can be used in your classroom whether you are a music teacher or classroom teacher.

For the Classroom Teacher

This first timeline, found on page 23, is for classroom teachers who would use this book as a means to enrich their classroom's language arts' curriculum. It is designed to give students a general idea of what it means to actively listen to music and then provides them with opportunities to listen to and then interpret the music.

Most of the mini-lessons used in the first timeline are designed to fit into a short amount of time (no longer than 15 minutes) so that they can fit into your day easily. Combine a couple of mini-lessons if you choose, change them or omit them to fit your teaching situation. The "Notes" are comments on how you may adapt things to fit your teaching needs. This plan was used in a 2nd grade classroom as well as a 5th grade classroom without much modification.

The plan for this timeline of lessons is outlined on page 23 and a blank plan sheet for your use can be found on page 45.

For the Music Teacher

The second example timeline, found on page 24, is meant for a music teacher who would use this book as a means to design a unit through active listening experiences. The unit plan first teaches students in depth what active listening is compared to passive and responsive and provides them with opportunities to listen and then talk intelligently about the music. There is also an assessment piece to this timeline. This plan was used in a 6th grade classroom; however, these lessons can be adaptable to any age group. For example, change the amount of vocabulary words you introduce or have students write the vocabulary words in sentences instead of a paragraph.

With this lesson timeline, you may want to give students their own Active Listening packet to use during the unit, which would include many or all of the reproducible papers sited in the table.

Lesson Timeline for a Classroom Teacher

#	Time minutes	Description	Ref Pg	Reproduc-ible Papers
1	8-10	Do "Music is Everywhere" activity.	25	29
2	15-20	Do "Teaching the 3 Types of Listening" activity.	25	30
3	5-8	Do "Sort out the Brainstorm" Note: Do this in partners.	26	29, bottom
4	8-10 min.	First Listening Experience: *Sabre Dance* by Aram Khachaturian. Listen, enjoy and get first impressions. Note: Don't tell the title of the piece yet. **Guided Qs:** What did you think of the piece? What did you imagine as you listened to the piece?	41	
5	During snack time	**Purpose:** Listen for overall mood and main character. **Use activity** #7 "Musical Faces" Note: Have students do the two-face paper: draw one face as the main character and the other face as any other character.	41 43	38
6		**Purpose:** Listen for more surprises, listen for parts of a narrative. Note: Model how I imagine character, setting, problem, solution. **Use activity** #5 "Creative Movement" Note: Do the mirror activity in partners. Students should move in a manner that the characters in the piece/story move. (For students who have extra time, let them draw a setting around their faces from yesterday.)	41 43	
7		**Purpose:** Listen for more details, differences in tempo and dynamics. **Use activity** #1 "Titles" Note: Have students write down their title ideas in a journal and keep them for later reference.	41 43	
8	10-12	Students are assigned and start cartoon. Note: Students may put unfinished cartoon in their folder to work on when they are finished with their morning work.	47-48, 52	49-51
9	30-45	Students share cartoon stories in groups and begin to write down their ideas in narrative format.	69	
10	Ongoing	Allow time for students to work on drafts of their stories.		
11		Publish and share stories.		

After you have done this cycle once, start it again using a different piece of music to write another story or a different type of writing like a poem or letter. A blank planning sheet for this can be found on page 45.

Lesson Timeline for a Music Teacher

#	40-45 min Classes	Description	Ref Pg	Reproducible Papers
1	1	Do "Music is Everywhere" activity. Do "Teaching the 3 Types of Listening" activity.	25 25	29 30
2	1	Have students do the "Illustrating the 3 Types of Listening" activity. Have students do the "Sort out the Brainstorm" activity. Check-up with "Which Way do they Listen?"	26 26 26	31 29, bottom 32
3	1	Do "Random Listening" activity. Do the "First Experience" activity using one of the pieces from "Random Listening."	26 26	
4 (op-tional)	1	Do "Analogies" activity. Do "How do You Listen?" questionnaire activity. Have "Composer, Performer, Listener" discussion, do journal entry.	27 27 27, 34	 33 35
5	2-3	Listening Experience: Cartoon project using *Sabre Dance* by Aram Khachaturian.	47-48, 52	49-51
6	1	Vocabulary – Go over the following words: composer, conductor, tempo, dynamics, forte, piano, sforzando, accent, crescendo, decrescendo, pitch, adagio, andante, allegro, vivace, etc. Use some familiar music to have students start using the words.	53	54
7	1	Vocabulary Activity – Play "Round Robin." Have students actively listen to Montagues and Capulets by Prokofiev. Have students orally practice using the vocabulary words.	55	
8	2	Vocabulary Practice – Have students do "Rate the Paragraph" activity. Have students get into partners and write a paragraph that uses 6 different vocabulary words correctly for Montagues and Capulets.	57	58 59,60
9	1	Administer test 1 on Listening. Introduce Performance Assessment, "Make a Performance Program." Have students start project. Assign due date.	 111	63 112-115
10	2-3	Allow work time on project.		
11	1	Share programs with class. Students complete rubric and pass in projects. Reflection Time – Make time for class discussion.	 122	 116-117

A modified assessment adapted for younger students can be found on pages 118-121.

Getting Your Students Ready to Listen

It is important for your students to become aware of the different ways we listen. The following activities have been developed so that you can introduce the concept of how we listen to your students. Music teachers may choose to teach all these activities in sequence in 3-4 classes. General classroom teachers may want to pick two or three activities that would work best to introduce the concepts to their students Both ways of using these activities are outlined in the lesson timelines on pages 23 and 24.

Activity Outlines

Day ONE

1. **Music is Everywhere (*Intro 8-10 min*)** Pass out paper and give students 30-45 seconds to brainstorm places where they would hear music playing. Then write some of their ideas on the board to share with the class. Some possible responses are:

NFL games	movie theaters	doctor's office
elevators	on hold	ice cream truck
hockey games	cell phones	theme parks
weddings	opera	airplane
radio	church	beach
mall	concerts	websites
bedroom	doorbell	bank
birthday parties	music store	dance
commercials	cars	restaurants

Ask them questions about these places: Do you listen to music the same way when you are in the doctor's office as when you are in a music store? in an elevator as at a dance? This sparks up a fun conversation and gets the kids thinking. For example, listening to music while you're on hold is a lot different than listening to music while at a concert. While on hold, your mind may wander, you may be annoyed with the person for whom you are holding, etc., (passive). However, if you are at a concert, you are probably singing or dancing or just enjoying the moment of the music (responsive).

Allow them time to complete the questions on the reproducible. Leave the last part for after students know the three types of listening.

2. **Teaching the 3 Types of Listening (*Information 15-20 min*)** Make three columns on the board and label the top of them respectively: Passive, Responsive, Active. Begin to explain what each one means and in each column write down some examples for each kind.

Here are a couple of ways you may want to teach this or to reinforce these concepts.
   - (Good for upper grades.) Pass out the informational reproducible (pages 30) and have your students read it silently or out loud. Follow up with a class discussion.
   - (Good for middle level grades.) Students can read the reproducible or have it read to them and then, in groups, choose a type of listening to demonstrate for the class in a 30-second skit or in a freeze frame. (A freeze frame is when a small group of students position themselves in a way that they are reacting to each other and demonstrating a concept.)

- (Good for lower grades.) You can demonstrate the three ways to listen to music while the class observes and reports on their observations. Notes can be kept on the board or in a journal for later reference. Students can then demonstrate a type of listening in a skit or freeze frame.

Day TWO
3. **Illustrating the 3 Types of Listening (*Follow-Up 10-15 min*)** Pass out the reproducible on page 31 and have students draw a person or people listening to music in each way. Students should add a caption sentence that goes with each illustration.

4. **Sort Out the Brainstorm (*Closure 5-8 min*)** Pick out a few of the places from your initial brainstorm where you hear music and determine how you would listen to music while there. Students should write down their ideas at the bottom of the "Music is Everywhere" paper. Be sure students tell why they chose the type of listening they did. You will find that we listen to music passively and responsively a lot more than actively. Be sure to bring this to the students' attention and let them know that they will be practicing their active listening skills in class.

Example: radio, responsive; "I like to sing when my favorite songs come on." commercials, passive; "Usually, I don't even notice that there is music playing during commercials." Internet music store, active; "I want to make sure I like the music I'm going to buy."

5. **Which Way do They Listen? (*Check-Up 5-8 min*)** The reproducible on page 32 can be used as a quiz or as an oral check up. Be sure to go over the answers after the quiz has been taken. This can be done at the end of day 2 or at the beginning of day 3.

Day THREE
6. **Random Listening** This is a great way to understand the differences among the ways in which we listen! Have students bring in some music and compile it with some of your own. (Be sure to let students know of the "day ahead" rule where they need to bring in their music a day ahead so that you have time to listen to it and give it your approval before playing it for the class.) Pick a piece of music at random and have students listen to it passively, responsively or actively.
   - Example: When asked to listen passively, the students' favorite song comes on, yet they try to force themselves to talk during it, even though they want to sing and dance while it plays.
   - Example: When asked to listen responsively, the students hear a slow, mournful melody played on the violin. Some students proceed to get up and make large dancing movements, other pretend to cry.
   - Example: When asked to listen actively, students sit and stroke their chins with their fingers as they ponder questions they ask aloud: "What does this music mean? I wonder why the instruments are playing so loudly...?"

7. **First Experience** At this point you intervene and give them their first experience with active listening. Because you are playing a song at random, you may have landed on a rock and roll or hip hop favorite. That's OK! Use it!
   Example: "I like the way you knew to start thinking about the music, but you were thinking so hard and out loud, that you forgot to listen. I'm going to start the music again and only play the first 30 seconds or so. Don't say anything until I stop the music, then you can raise your hand and talk about anything you heard."

Play the introduction to the music for about the first 20-30 seconds and stop it. Students will have a lot to say about the music. Use this time to experiment by playing more of the piece or going on to a new one. This would also be a great time to model how YOU listen actively.

Day FOUR (optional)

8. **Analogies** "Listening to music is like…" These analogy exercises can help your students to understand why people take the time to actively listen to and enjoy music.
   - Eating – Give each of your students a piece of chocolate but don't let them eat it until you have given them a task to do (read a passage in a book, sharpen their pencils, find a folder in their desk). When they start to do their task, they can eat their chocolate. After they are done, ask them if they enjoyed the candy. Then ask them to really think about it. Did they really get to enjoy the smooth, sweet taste of the candy on their pallet or did they eat it quickly while their mind was on completing their task?
   - Artwork – Find an interesting piece of artwork (a colorful painting, something abstract). Tell the students that you will show them the artwork and ask them to make as many comments as possible about the artwork. When students are ready, show them the artwork for about 2 seconds only and ask them what they thought. You will get a couple of observations, but not much.

   In both cases, emphasize that in order to really enjoy something, you need to focus on it. You may want to follow these up by giving the students another piece of chocolate to really enjoy or allow students to look at the intricacies of the artwork. Their comments will be abundant this time. Make sure you parallel these experiences to listening to music. Only when they focus on the music, will they be able to really enjoy it.

9. **How do You Listen?** Have students complete this little questionnaire on page 33 orally or in written form and use it as a springboard for a class discussion.

10. **Composer, Performer, Listener** The full quote by modern composer William Schuman on page 34 is for you. Use the handout on page 35 as a means to discuss the three important people that are involved with all music. Then, allow some time for students to write their own personal answers.

POSTERS
Use the two posters on pages 36 and 37 for your room.

EXTENTIONS
- Students write a paragraph, an article, or make a Power Point presentation that explains the three types of listening
- Have students make a questionnaire or a poll to see how people listen to music; graph the results.

Active Listening

Inspiring Our Ears As We Listen!

Name:

_____

Class:

_____

Date Started:

_____

Name: _____ Class: _____ Date: _____

Music is Everywhere!

1. List as many places as you can where you find music playing.

   _____   _____

   _____   _____

   _____   _____

   _____   _____

   _____   _____

   _____   _____

2. Pick two places from your list that are very different from each other and write them
   here. _____   _____

3. Explain how you listen to music differently at these two places. _____
   _____
   _____

4. Pick two places where you would listen to music in a similar way.. Write them here.

   _____   _____

5. Explain how you listen to music similarly at these two places. _____
   _____
   _____

6. Pick either the answers for #2 or #4 and draw a picture of each place on the back of this
   paper or on a separate piece of paper.

7. (To be done later.) Sort out some of the places from your list into the 3 columns.

Passively	Responsively	Actively

Three Types of Listening

There are many ways in which one can listen to music. Just think about some people you know and you may find that each one listens to music differently. There's the young child who dances to music played at an outside concert in the park, the couple who eats a candlelit dinner to classical music, the teenage boy who blares music through his speakers in his room, the young girl who cries at the sound of a love song, the person who listens to the radio in the car … the list could go on and on. Think of when and how you listen to music. Is it when you are alone with an MP3 player or while you are doing chores around the house? Though there are many different situations in which we can listen to music, there are only three basic ways to listen to music: **passively**, **responsively**, and **actively**.

When listening **passively**, one is not really paying attention to the music. Instead, the music is in the **background**. Have you ever sat down to read a book for pleasure or as an assignment and your mind wandered to other things: the conversation next to you, something you need to get done, your growling stomach, or things you'd rather be doing? When you get back to the book, you find you're on the next page – but you haven't absorbed a word you just "read." You have blocked out the meaning behind the words. That's exactly what happens when you have music on and you're doing homework, reading, or talking with a friend. The music goes in one ear and out the other.

Have you ever had a real suspenseful story read to you? Usually you respond to what you hear. When you get to a part you're really interested in, you might start to lean in to listen more carefully. Some people's eyes get wide as they wait for the next details in the story. When people listen **responsively** to music they may respond by bobbing their head, tapping their foot, dancing, or singing. There are many places where people listen responsively: at a concert, at a dance, or at a party, for example. When someone listens responsively, the music creates an **atmosphere** for the listener. Take a dance, for example. The DJ creates the atmosphere for the dance by the music he plays. If he wants to get people dancing, then he will play a popular, upbeat song that's easy to dance to. If he wants to calm the dancers down before it's time to go home, he will play a slow song. All the while, the DJ controls the atmosphere by playing certain songs. The dancers are the ones who listen responsively by responding to the music. Athletes sometimes will pump themselves up before a game by playing music that has a fast tempo. At other times, a person who has had a hard day, might play something that relaxes him. The responsive listener likes to be surrounded by the sounds of music and responds to it in some way.

When someone is reading a book to find out answers to things, that person is actively reading. He is discovering new things and thinking about what he reads. **Actively** listening to music is when the music is the main focus and the listener is really **thinking** about the music. Sometimes, people actively listen when they are trying to learn or understand the lyrics of a song. At other times, active listeners want to study the melody of a song, so that they can play it on an instrument. Often when people actively listen to music, they will imagine stories that are happening inside the music or even relate the music to their own lives.

Many people have the opportunity to listen passively and responsively, but not actively. The next time you hear music, stop and think about it while it plays. You may be surprised at what you hear!

Three Types of Listening

Draw a picture of people listening in these three ways. Write down a caption that tells what they are doing.

Passive	Responsive	Active

_____ _____ _____
_____ _____ _____
_____ _____ _____

Which Way Do They Listen?

There are three main ways in which we listen to music: passively, responsively and actively. The person who listens passively does things while music is on in the background and isn't really listening to the music. A responsive listener plays music to create an atmosphere. When a person is actively listening to music, he/she is listening to the details of the music and thinking about them. Below are some examples of how people listen. See if you can determine how they are listening. Put P for Passive, R for Responsive and A for Active.

1. ____ John is getting ready for his football game and is listening to music that helps pump him up.
2. ____ Mrs. Jones has music playing while she and her husband have an anniversary dinner.
3. ____ Ken's sister is practicing a piece of music on the piano while he talks on the phone to his friend. How is Ken listening?
4. ____ Zach is trying to figure out the lyrics to his favorite song so he can understand what the song really means.
5. ____ Brad taps along to the rhythm of his favorite song and notices that the drummer plays a lot of complicated rhythms. He even tries to imitate them.
6. ____ Sara just broke up with her boyfriend and is listening to sad music in her bedroom.
7. ____ It's three days before his concert and Mr. Nu is listening to a recording of himself playing the violin.
8. ____ Sue listens to a song on the internet before she buys it to make sure she likes the music.
9. ____ Madeline jumps at the dramatic music being played during the horror film.
10. ____ Mrs. Bedrosian is listening to her chorus practice a piece of music for the spring concert.
11. ____ Jill, Bethany and Madeline are dancing up a storm at the semi formal.
12. ____ Brett is trying hard to finish up his math homework while he listens to the radio.
13. ____ Jack notices that although the words to the chorus of his favorite song change, the melody doesn't.
14. ____ Music is playing while Sean sits in a chair waiting for the dentist to come back with the drill.

What is your favorite way to listen to music? Why? _____

_____

_____

_____

_____

Inspired by Listening

How Do You Listen?

1. When eating dinner, do you ...
    a. always listen to music?
    b. listen to music every once in a while?
    c. never listen to music?
2. When at a school dance, do you
    a. mostly talk to your friends?
    b. dance, dance, and dance some more?
    c. talk to your friends and dance some too?
3. When you do your homework, do you
    a. listen to music to help you work better?
    b. listen to music to drown out other noises?
    c. never listen to music?
4. When doing chores around the house, do you
    a. listen to music to help you work faster?
    b. sometimes have music on in the background?
    c. never listen to music?
5. When listening to the radio, CDs or MP3s do you
    a. often sing along to familiar songs?
    b. let your mind wander to other things?
    c. listen for new things in the song (lyrics, guitar riff)?
6. When at a concert, do you like to
    a. dance and sing?
    b. let your mind wander?
    c. focus on what the musicians are doing?
7. What is your favorite song? _____
    What are at least 4 things you can tell other people about that song?

- _____
- _____
- _____
- _____
- _____
- _____

Active Listening is Important!

"It is revealing to compare the actions of theater audiences to those of symphonic audiences. In the theater the audience listens with full attention to every line of the play, knowing that if important lines are missed understanding can be diminished – this instinctive attention is too often lacking in the concert hall. One has but to observe listeners at a concert to witness the distractions of talking or reading or simply staring into space. Only a small percentage is vitally concerned with the essential role of active listening. This lack is serious because the listener is essential to the process of music; music after all consists of the composer, the performer, and the listener. Each of these three elements should be present in the most ideal way. We expect a fine composition brilliantly performed, but how often do we think that it should also be brilliantly heard?"

-William Schuman

The listener is a vital part of the musical equation.

Composer, Performer and Listener

"… the listener is essential to the process of music; music after all consists of the composer, the performer, and the listener. Each of these three elements should be present in the most ideal way."

-William Schuman

Journal Entry: What are the roles of composer, performer and listener? Are any of these roles more important than the others? Why or why not?

_____

_____

_____

_____

_____

_____

_____

Get Ready to Listen!

1. Clear your area.

2. Get comfortable.

3. Clear your mind.

4. Listen and enjoy.

Active Listeners Ask ...

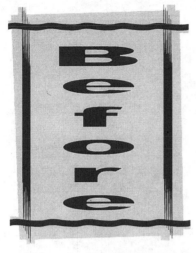

What is the title of this piece?
Do I know who composed this piece
 of music?
Do I know when in history this piece
 was composed?
Do I know why this piece was
 composed?

What do I think of this music?
What instruments do I hear?
Are there any surprises in the music?
What is the **tempo**?
What are the **dynamics**?
Are there different sections to this
 piece?
Are there any repeating sections in
 this piece?

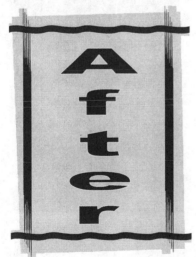

What did I think of the music?
What parts did I like?
What did I imagine was happening in
 the music?
What was the overall mood of the
 piece?

Your BRAIN is active
when you are Actively Listening!

Name: _____

Class: _____ Date: _____

Musical Faces

Inspired by: _____

by: _____

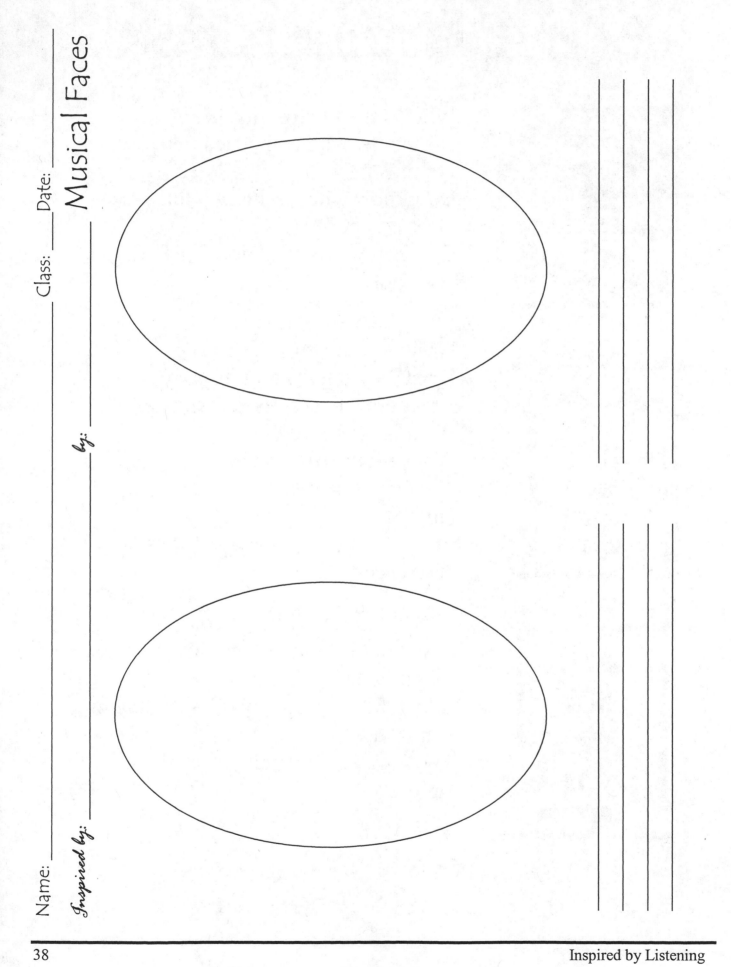

Name: _____

Class: _____ Date: _____

Musical Faces

Inspired by: _____ *by:* _____

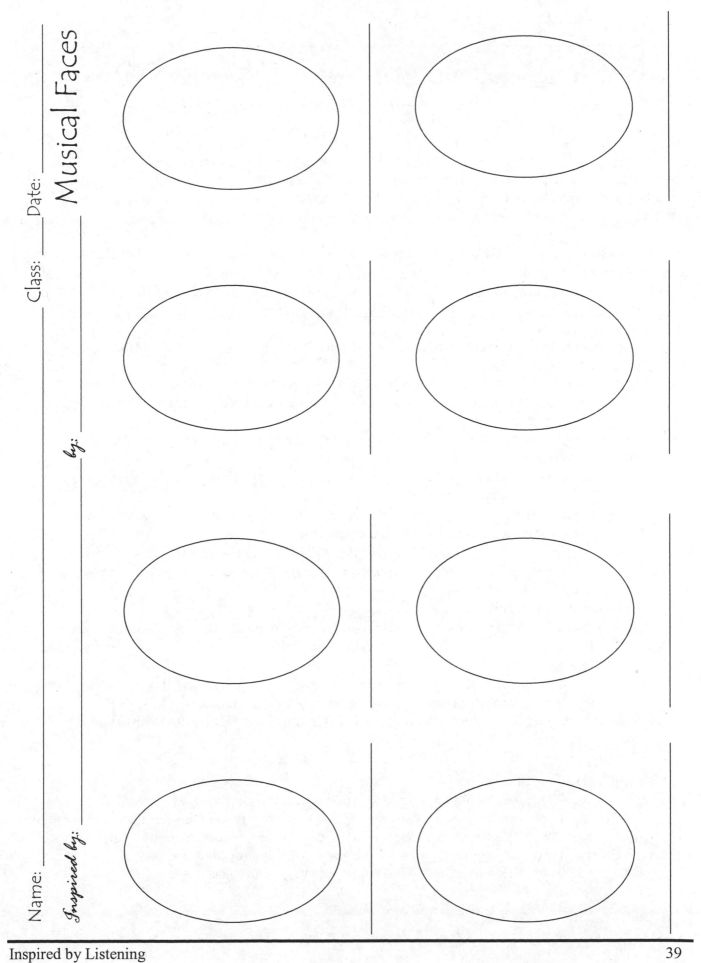

The Active Listening Experience

Once your students are familiar with what it means to actively listen, they are ready for their first listening experience. I refer to them as experiences because there is so much you can do with them. It's like you are taking your students on a mini-field trip and then using that experience to further enhance your teaching.

In Part 1, there was an overview on how to conduct an Active Listening Experience. Let's look again at what needs to happen in order to conduct meaningful listening experiences.

1. First, you must **plan ahead**. You do this by picking out music and deciding what you want to do with it: learn music vocabulary, write stories, learn about history, etc. See page 45 for a planning sheet you can use.

2. Next, your students need to have their **first listening**. At this time you get students' first impressions and opinions.

3. Once this happens, you need to allow time for **repetitive listenings.** Allowing for this time is important to keep students interested and listening. Students need repetition in order to experience a piece of music fully.

4. Use some of the following to help you **focus** your listening experiences. Examples can be found on the following pages.
   - *Setting Purposes* (page 41) – Set a purpose before each time you play the piece of music. This gives students a motivation to listen again.
   - *Guided Questions* (page 41) – These should be used often to encourage students to talk about the music and think intelligently about it.
   - *Activities* (page 43-44) – Short activities will help solidify your students' listening experiences. These should be fun and engaging. They can be tailored to fit your students' ages, talents and needs.

5. Get you students to **reflect** in a journal.
   - Journal Entries (page 42) – Use journal prompts to get students to talk further about their listening experiences. This can also be a great place to jot down ideas to use in future lessons.
   - Another idea is to have your students to keep a "first impressions" journal where they write their first impressions of each piece of music they experience.

6. Integrate the experiences further into your curriculum by using them as an **inspirational springboard** from which to base another assignment.

Collaborating on the Listening Experience

If you are a music teacher, you could be the one to introduce the musical concepts as well as the music itself while the classroom teacher could follow up and allow time for repetitive listenings and/or use the experiences to base a writing assignment. Meanwhile, the music teacher could continue to work on the same (or a different) piece to emphasize musical concepts. Working together this way is great. It allows both teachers to focus on different aspects of an active listening experience.

SETTING PURPOSES

As students become familiar with a piece of music, they should begin to listen intelligently to it. The teacher aids in this process by **setting purposes** for listening. These should draw their attention to the music itself. Here are some ideas. Don't limit yourself to this list, in fact add to it as you discover ideas that suit your needs and style.

1. Listen for more details.
2. Listen for surprises.
3. Listen for melody, sing it.
4. Listen for harmony, sing it.
5. Listen for differences in tempo (musical speed).
6. Listen for differences in dynamics (loud and soft).
7. Listen for certain instruments (tone color).
8. Count how many different sections there are in a piece.
9. Listen for the main theme of the piece (the one that is most familiar and often repeated).
10. Count how many times you hear the same theme.
11. Listen for the rhythm pattern/motif.
12. Count how many times the rhythm pattern/motif repeats itself in the piece or section.
13. _____
14. _____
15. _____

GUIDED QUESTIONS

Here are some example questions to ask your class while you are still experiencing a piece of music. They will prompt them to respond to the music both intelligently and emotionally. These questions should draw their attention to how they feel about the music and get them to start interpreting the music by gaining their own opinions about it. Again add to this list as you think of more ideas.

1. Do you like the piece? Why or why not?
2. What do you think of the music?
3. What parts do you like? Why?
4. What parts don't you like? Why?
5. Raise your hand to show who likes the piece/this section/etc.
6. What does the music sound like?
7. What do you picture/imagine when the music is playing?
8. How do you feel when the music is playing?
9. What do you think the composer was thinking when he wrote this?
10. Why do you think the composer used this/these particular instrument(s)?
11. Why do you think this piece was written?
12. _____
13. _____
14. _____
15. _____

JOURNAL ENTRY IDEAS

Use these as a means for your students to reflect on their experiences more deeply. You may also want to use journals to gather first impressions about music as students listen.

1. Some people compare listening to music with looking at a painting. In what ways are the two similar? In what ways are they different?
2. What are the roles of composer, performer and listener? Are any of these roles more important than the others? Why or why not?
3. What job would you rather have: that of composer, performer or listener? Why?
4. If you could only listen to music in one way for a year, which way would you choose? Why?
5. If you could only listen to one genre of music for one year, which genre would you choose? Why?
6. If you could only listen to one band's, artist's or composer's music for one year, which would you choose? Why?
7. Is there a song you could listen to over and over? What is it? Why could you listen to it repetitively?
8. What is your favorite piece of music to listen to? Why?
9. What is your least favorite piece of music to listen to? Why?
10. What is your favorite/least favorite genre of music to listen to? Why?
11. Where do you like to listen to music? Why?
12. What would be the most perfect setting to listen to music? Why?
13. How is listening to music like reading a book?
14. If you had to compose a piece of music that other students would have to listen to passively, describe the kind of music you would compose. Why would you compose it that way?
15. If you had to compose a piece of music that other students would have to listen to responsively, describe the kind of music you would compose. Why would you compose it that way?
16. If you had to compose a piece of music that other students would have to listen to actively, describe the kind of music you would compose. Why would you compose it that way?
17. Describe the most perfect types of music to listen to passively, responsively and actively. What makes them that way?
18. Describe the least perfect types of music to listen to passively, responsively and actively. What makes them that way?
19. _____
   _____
20. _____
   _____
21. _____
   _____

ACTIVITIES

These activities are designed to help students develop active listening skills by engaging them in more active learning. They cater to students' different learning styles. Use what's best for your classroom and don't be afraid to use the same one multiple times. Students will benefit from doing similar activities using different music.

1. **Titles** Before telling the students the title of a piece, have students suggest good titles after listening to it. Ask why they chose those titles. Tell students the title of the piece and ask why they think the composer chose such a title.

2. **Words and Phrases** Students individually, in groups or as a class brainstorm a list of words and/or phrases they think of when listening to or thinking about the piece. This list can be kept in a journal for future reference in their writing. Share and discuss afterwards. Use the "Word/Doodle Boxes" on page 92 to have students write down ideas for sections of a piece or for whole pieces of music.

3. **Key Words** Students individually, in groups or as a class brainstorm a list of words they think of when listening to or thinking about the piece. This list of words is then narrowed down to a list of six key words that can be kept on an index card or in a journal. After doing this for a few pieces, the students can use these sets of key words to differentiate among the pieces. They can quiz each other or the teacher may make up a key word quiz for them. This is also used well with composers where students find the key words for the composers they are studying, making the differences among them clearer. (see pages 134-135)

4. **Sentences** Students write sentences about what is going on in the music. These may be descriptions of the music itself or of what they imagine to be happening. These sentences may be the beginnings to stories or endings to stories. Use these sentences in groups and have students build stories from them. Have students take all the sentences and put them into piles for good beginnings, middles and ends to stories.

5. **Creative Movement** Allow students time to move freely and creatively to a piece of music. You may also put variations to this: move while sitting, move only your arms, move with your eyes closed, move with a friend, mirror a friend, move only your fingers and toes, etc. Discuss afterwards.

6. **Facial Movement** Students move to the music with only facial expressions to show the personality of the piece, instruments etc. Discuss afterwards.

7. **Musical Faces** Students draw or make visual representations of faces as a response to the music or that of a section of the piece. (see pages 38-39) These faces usually show the overall mood of the piece. They can also represent a character that the student imagines as they listen to the piece. Use these characters to write stories, letters, monologues, etc. Share and discuss afterwards.

8. **Musical Doodles** Have students make doodles of the music they hear. The music leads the pencil so that the doodles represent how the music sounds. Do this on scrap paper or on register tape to show the progression of the music. Share and discuss afterwards. Use the "Word/Doodle Boxes" on page 92 to have students doodle ideas for sections of a piece or for whole pieces of music.

9. **Free Draw** After listening to a piece, have students draw what they imagine. Share and discuss afterwards.

10. **Musical Quilt** Have students do a free draw for a piece of music on uniform pieces of paper. When done, arrange these papers into a quilt and attach them together with yarn or tape. Hang the quilt on a bulletin board. Make different quilts using different pieces of music. Hang them side by side to compare.

11. **Cartoon Sequence** Students draw a cartoon sequence of 4 or more panels that illustrate a story they hear in the music. See the complete lesson plan starting on page 47. The reproducible is on page 49.

12. **Sequence of Events** Using the same idea as the cartoon, students draw a sequence of events that go with the music. Reproducibles can be found on pages 78 and 79.

EXTENSIONS
- Write a story using the ideas that came from the cartoon, sequence of events, sentences or free draw.
- Using the words or key words students came up with; write a poem about the music.
- Make a doll or create a character that illustrates the facial expressions used in musical faces or facial movement. Make this character the main character of a story or have them write a letter in the point of view of the character.
- Make a skit that demonstrates the story heard in the music.

The following plan on page 45 is great for general classroom teachers to use as well as music teachers. Use this to help organize meaningful activities that focus your purposes for listening. An example has been filled in on page 46.

Class: _____ Date: _____

PLANNING AN ACTIVE LISTENING EXPERIENCE
Use this to help you plan a listening experience for any piece of music.

Plan Ahead:
Music to be Used: _____
Future Plans: _____

First Listening:
When and Where: _____
Get First Impressions: _____

Repetitive Listenings:
When and Where: _____

Purpose for Listening: _____
Activity: _____
Special Notes: _____

Purpose for Listening: _____
Activity: _____
Special Notes: _____

Purpose for Listening: _____
Activity: _____
Special Notes: _____

Extension Ideas: _____

_____

Student Reflection:
Journal Entry: _____

Other Resources/Ideas:

_____

_____

Class: _____Example Class Plan_____ Date: _____

PLANNING AN ACTIVE LISTENING EXPERIENCE
Use this to help you plan a listening experience for any piece of music.

Plan Ahead:
Music to be Used: _____Tuxedo Junction by Glenn Miller_____

Future Plans: _____Write Poetry_____

First Listening:
When and Where: _____During Snack on Monday, lights off but shades up____

Get First Impressions: _____Q: what did you think? How did the music make you feel?____

Repetitive Listenings:
When and Where: _____During Snack on Tues, Wed, Thurs_____

Purpose for Listening: _____Listen for surprises and details in the music_____

Activity: _____Facial Movement, sitting at desks_____

Special Notes: _____Let the music "move your face" for you; How does the music make you feel?____

Purpose for Listening: _____Listen for action in the music_____

Activity: _____Musical Doodles_____

Special Notes: _____Let the pencil do the actions in the music_____

Purpose for Listening: _Listen for details and layering in the music; things you missed before_

Activity: _____Words and Phrases_____

Special Notes: _____Focus on verbs_____

Extension Ideas: _____Create a DADA poem using the words and phrases. *Copy DADA poetry worksheet. (p. 102) Do this on FRIDAY!_____

Student Reflection:
Journal Entry: _____How do you think the composer felt when he/she wrote this?____

Other Resources/Ideas:
_____Offer option to do free form poetry using some of the words and phrases students came up with. Do this with another piece and compare the poems along with the music!_____

Detailed Plan for Activity #11...Make a Cartoon!

The following lesson is designed to motivate students as they listen to an exciting piece of music. This has been used in elementary and middle school classrooms with great success. There are two example rubrics included to show the adaptability to different age levels.

Lesson Summary: Students will create a cartoon as an interpretation of a piece of music.

Overall Objectives:
STUDENTS WILL:
- Actively listen to an exciting piece of music.
- Create a visual representation of their interpretation of the piece.

Complimentary Standards: Narratives: setting, character, plot
                          Visual Art: cartooning, drawing, painting, etc.

Time: 3 class periods or about 1½ - 2 hours

Layout of Classroom: Students will need areas to do paper and pencil work

Materials and Preparation:

Teacher	Student
Recording of exciting piece of music	Pencil
Suggestions:	Cartoon reproducible page 49
Sabre Dance by Khachaturian	Coloring utensils
Rite of Spring by Stravinsky	

Procedures:

Day One
1. Get students ready by introducing the piece to them. (Sometimes it's good to tell the title of the piece from the beginning and other times it's fun to let the piece speak for itself. I've done it both ways; both work fine.)
2. Have students get into their "active listening stance" and play the piece once.
3. When done, get some students' first impressions.
4. Before playing the piece again, give the students a purpose for listening: "Close your eyes, enjoy the piece of music and see what kinds of images come to mind."
5. Play the piece again and then have them give some of their ideas afterwards.
6. Before playing the piece for a third time, give students a new purpose for listening: "This time when you listen, think about the story that is developing in your head.
   - Who are the characters in the story?
   - What do they look like?
   - Where are they?
   - What are they doing?"

7. Play the piece again and have students give some of their ideas.
8. Explain to students the assignment: "Draw a four panel cartoon that goes along with the story that developed in your head as you listened to the piece."
9. If time allows, have students set up their papers and start the assignment or listen to the piece again with the assignment in mind.

Day Two (You may find that you do not need to commit a full class period to working on this.)
1. Remind students of the assignment and play the piece as a refresher.
2. Allow time for students to work on their cartoon. Play the piece while students work.

Day Three
1. Allow students time to share their cartoons with others. This can be done in pairs, small groups or as a whole class.
2. Have students fill in their rubrics for the cartoon.

Reflection Questions/Journal Entry Ideas:
* Was it easy or difficult to draw an interpretation of a piece of music?
* Who felt comfortable doing this, who didn't? Why?

Assessment Tool: Rubric page 50 for older students, page 51 for younger students

Extensions:
* Have students turn the cartoon into a written narrative.
* Have students act out a cartoon (theirs or a friend's).
* Make a class book of cartoons.

Name: _____ Class: _____ Date: _____

Musical Cartoon

Inspired by: _____ *by:* _____

Rubric for Cartoon

Use this rubric to help you do the best job you can do!

When you are done with your final copy, complete the self-assessment section of this rubric. Pass this in with your final copy.

Criteria	Level 1	Level 2	Level 3	Level 4
Content	The 4 panels are not all complete. It is hard to tell if the illustrations represent the piece of music.	The 4 panels are somewhat complete in content. Illustrations somewhat represent the piece of music.	There are 4 complete panels to the cartoon. Illustrations effectively represent the piece of music.	There are 4 complete panels to the cartoon. Illustrations very effectively represent the different sections of the piece of music.
Appearance	Illustrations are not neat or complete. They are not in color.	Illustrations are somewhat neat and complete. They are in color.	Illustrations are neat, complete and in color.	Illustrations are neat, complete, in color and have a lot of detail.

Assessment

Criteria	Self-Assessment	Teacher-Assessment
Content	Circle one: 1 2 3 4	Circle one: 1 2 3 4
Appearance	Circle one: 1 2 3 4	Circle one: 1 2 3 4

Student Comments: (Write at least one comment about your work.)

_____

_____ Total_____out of 8 points.

Teacher Comments

_____

_____ Total_____out of 8 points.

Name: _____ Class: _____ Date: _____

Rubric for Cartoon

Color in the face that goes with how you feel you did.

1. I have four panels in my cartoon.

    Great Job!   OK   Needs Work

2. The cartoon tells the story in the music.

    Great Job!   OK   Needs Work

3. My cartoon is done neatly.

    Great Job!   OK   Needs Work

4. My cartoon is done in color.

    Great Job!   OK   Needs Work

Example Cartoon
Inspired by: Sabre Dance
by: Aram Khachaturian

Music Vocabulary

What better way to understand musical terms than to learn them as you listen to music? The following terms are a few that you may want to use. As you listen more and more to different music, you and your students may want to add words to the list.

The activities starting on page 55 are great for music teachers. They will help students learn and use these words as they actively listen in order to analyze and understand music.

melody	the "tune," the part of the music you hum
harmony	when two or more notes are heard at the same time
rhythm	pattern of movement through a piece of music; beat is the steady pulse of a piece
tone color	an instrument's own special sound; what makes each instrument unique
form	how a piece is constructed Examples: intro, verse, chorus, verse, chorus, bridge, guitar solo, chorus, ending; differing sections of an instrumental piece; ABA
dynamics	volume of music
piano	(p) soft
forte	(f) loud
	pp, p, mp, mf, f, ff (from softest to loudest)
crescendo	gradually get louder
decrescendo	gradually get softer
pitch	the high and low sounds of music
tempo	speed of music
adagio	slow
andante	at a walking pace
allegro	quick
vivace	fast
accent	(<) a short sudden note
sfortzando	(sf) a forced sound
dissonance	a combination of sounds that are disagreeable to the ear
resolution	when dissonant notes transition and become pleasing to the ear
composer	a person who writes music
conductor	a person who directs a group of musicians
score	the written form of a musical composition
solo	one person performing alone on an instrument or with his/her voice
orchestra	many people performing on instruments
concerto	an orchestral piece that features a soloist
chorus	many people performing with their voices
improvisation	composing on the spot without any preparation; making it up as you go

Music Vocabulary

melody	
harmony	
rhythm	
tone color	
form	
dynamics	
piano	
forte	
crescendo	
decrescendo	
pitch	
tempo	
adagio	
andante	
allegro	
vivace	
accent	
sfortzando	
dissonance	
resolution	
composer	
conductor	
score	
solo	
orchestra	
concerto	
chorus	
improvisation	

SUGGESTIONS FOR INTRODUCING VOCABULARY

- Pass out blank vocabulary table (page 54) and have students fill in definitions.
- Go over only a few vocabulary words at a time. These do NOT have to be done in order nor do you have to go over all of them.
- Listen to sample excerpts so that students can practice using the words.

ACTIVITIES TO PRACTICE THE VOCABULARY

Working with the vocabulary words:

- Make *flash cards*
  Have students make flash cards out of index cards. Put a word on one side of the card and the definition on the other. Use these to test your class or for them to test each other.
- Make *round robin cards*
  These are similar to flash cards, but they can be used for a whole class activity.
  How to make them:
    1. Write a vocabulary word on one side of an index card. Label only this card with a number 1.
    2. On a different card, write the definition on one side and a different vocabulary word on the other side.
    3. Continue with another index card by writing the definition of the second word on one side and a third word on the other side.
    4. Continue writing these cards in this "chain-like" fashion.
    5. When you are done with the last word, write its definition on the back of the first card you wrote which will have the first vocabulary word.

Card One, front   Card One, back

| DYNAMICS | Person who writes |
| 1 | music |

Card Two, front   Card Two, back

| volume in music | TEMPO |

Card Three, front   Card Three, back

| speed in music | COMPOSER |

How to use them:
  1. Pass out the cards in a random order to your class. If there are extra cards, give some of your students two to use.

2. The student who has the card with the number 1 starts.
3. He/she says the vocabulary word on the card. The student who has the definition for that word, reads the definition out loud.
4. Then that student turns the card over and says the vocabulary word that is on the back and whoever has the definition, reads it out loud.
5. This continues until all the words and definitions have been read.
6. When they are done, you may collect the cards and redistribute them so that everyone has a different card OR you can do the same game again and see how fast they can get through the cards.

- Play *vocabulary bingo*
  With this activity, students will make their own bingo cards to play the traditional game.
  How to make and use them:
  1. Give students a blank bingo card (or a blank piece of paper) that is (or can) be divided into 9-12 boxes.
  2. In each box, have students write a vocabulary word.
  3. To play, read off the definitions and if any student has that word on their card, they cover it or cross it out.
  4. The first student to cover a row, column, four corners or the whole board, (depending on the game) wins!

Practicing the vocabulary words:

- *Model good vocabulary usage*
  Orally MODEL how to use the vocabulary words. Use the same "thinking out loud" method described on page 16. This time, however, when you stop the music, use the vocabulary you are trying to reinforce. Again, plan ahead! Using music you know will allow you to use the vocabulary words you have given your students and plan out what types of things you will say. It is all right to have a paper with you to which you can refer as you "think out loud." Remember, this is the time for students to observe you as you model active listening behaviors. They do not need to contribute - yet!

- *Give your students a chance*
  Once you have modeled how to use vocabulary words, allow your students to interject during the times you stop the music. Guide them as they try out the new words. Correct them and encourage them.

- *The hardest part*
  The hardest part of vocabulary usage for emerging active listeners is describing where in the music they hear the things they hear. This is why modeling and planning what you will say ahead of time is so important. For example, a student may know that there is a crescendo in the piece, but they do not know how to put that into words in terms of the context of the piece. Guide them by asking questions such as:
    o Did you hear that in the beginning/middle/end of the section/piece?
    o What instrument played the crescendo?
    o Did you hear it in the melody or in the harmony parts?
    o Was there one big crescendo that stood out in the excerpt/piece?

When in doubt, you may want to play the excerpt again so that the student(s) can listen more intently for the answer.

ACTIVITIES TO USE THE VOCABULARY WORDS

Vocabulary Cards (Good for emerging and/or younger listeners)

For this activity, students listen to a piece of music and write down 6 vocabulary words they can use to describe the piece; one word on each index card. From there, you can:

- Have students stand in front of the class and explain why they chose that word.
- Have students gather in groups to share the reasons why they chose those words.
- Collect all the cards, tally and graph the vocabulary words used. Have the class discuss why the words were chosen and why some were chosen more than others.
- Have students draw a representation of the vocabulary word on the back of the card as it relates to the music.
- Have students choose a word or two to act out as it relates to the music. (Vocabulary Charades, anyone?)

Write a Paragraph (Good for more advanced and/or older listeners)

The following is a brief description of an assignment, some example paragraphs that show the differing levels of achievement according to the rubric, and a rubric to use for the assignment.

Suggested Procedure: (Time: 2-3 classes)
1. Introduce the assignment of writing a paragraph using the vocabulary.
2. Hand out the rubric you will be using (page 60) and go over it.
3. Show students example paragraphs and have students rate the paragraphs according to the rubric. Talk about what is good and what needs improvement in each paragraph. (page 58)
4. Pair students up to try their own paragraphs using a new piece of music. (page 59)

Example Paragraphs: These example paragraphs have been written for *Sabre Dance* by Aram Khachaturian, which is a suggested piece used for the cartoon assignment on page 47. The paragraphs are arranged from the lowest level to the highest.

> This paragraph is about the *Sabre Dance*. It begins with loud noises. It has a fast tempo. It has pitch. There are a lot of dynamics in it. There are crescendos and decrescendos. I like the *Sabre Dance*.

> The *Sabre Dance* is a song we listened to in music. It has a fast tempo except for the middle part. There are high and low pitches. There is a crescendo where the dynamics go from soft to loud. There is a lot of forte. The *Sabre Dance* is fun to listen to.

> The *Sabre Dance* is a great song. It has a fast tempo throughout the piece. It is mostly forte. There are many accents in the piece. Also, the high and low pitches in the song seem to be playing against each other. I picture a circus where there are a lot of clowns.

> The *Sabre Dance* is a fun piece of music to listen to. It has a fast tempo throughout the song. It begins with low pitched, forte notes. After those notes, there are very fast, high pitched notes that make me think of running feet. There are many accents in this piece that help make it sound lively and exciting. The ending of the piece is made up of decrescendo, followed by a crescendo and finally an accent. This piece makes me think of a lively chase where a person is being chased by a robber.

Other Suggested Pieces to Use for this Assignment: *Montagues and Capulets* by Prokofiev; *Ride of the Valkyries* by Wagner; *Rite of Spring* by Stravinsky; *Pastoral Symphony* by Beethoven. (You may want to use excerpts of these pieces instead of the full piece of music.)

Rate the Paragraph

Read each paragraph, write down what is good, what needs improvement and finally, rate the paragraph using the rubric.

Inspired by: *Sabre Dance* *by*: Aram Khacaturian

	THINGS THAT ARE GOOD	WHAT NEEDS IMPROVEMENT	THE RATING
The *Sabre Dance* is a song we listened to in music. It has a fast tempo except for the middle part. There are high and low pitches. There is a crescendo where the dynamics go from soft to loud. There is a lot of forte. The *Sabre Dance* is fun to listen to.			
The *Sabre Dance* is a great song. It has a fast tempo throughout the piece. It is mostly forte. There are many accents in the piece. Also, the high and low pitches in the song seem to be playing against each other. I picture a circus where there are a lot of clowns.			
This paragraph is about the *Sabre Dance*. It begins with loud noises. It has a fast tempo. It has pitch. There are a lot of dynamics in it. There are crescendos and decrescendos. I like the *Sabre Dance*.			
The *Sabre Dance* is a fun piece of music to listen to. It has a fast tempo throughout the piece. It begins with low pitched, forte notes. After those notes, there are very fast, high pitched notes that make me think of running feet. There are many accents in this piece that help make it sound lively and exciting. The ending of the piece is made up of decrescendo, followed by a crescendo and finally an accent. This piece makes me think of a lively chase where a person is being chased by a robber.			

Name(s): _____ Class: _____ Date: _____

Musical Paragraph

Inspired by: _____ *by:* _____

Topic Sentence: _____

_____

Detail Sentences (use 6 different vocabulary words)

1. _____

_____

2. _____

_____

3. _____

_____

4. _____

_____

5. _____

_____

6. _____

_____

Closing Sentence: _____

_____

Draw a picture to go with your paragraph.

Name(s): _____ Class: _____ Date: _____

Rubric for Paragraph

Use this rubric to help you do the best job you can do! When you are done with your first draft, have someone read what you have and help you determine where you are in your progress. Make changes as necessary and then complete your final copy.

When you are done with your final copy, complete the self-assessment section of this rubric. Pass this in with your final copy.

Criteria	Level 1	Level 2	Level 3	Level 4
Vocabulary Usage	Most of the vocab words are not used correctly or there is little evidence that the writer knows the meaning of the words.	At least 3-5 vocab words are used somewhat correctly. Other vocab words are not used correctly or there is little evidence that the writer knows the meaning of the words.	At least 5 vocab words are used somewhat correctly.	All 6 vocab words are used correctly.
Examples	There are ineffective examples of what the listener thinks of when he/she hears the piece or there are no examples.	There are moderately effective examples of what the listener thinks of when he/she hears the piece.	There are effective examples of what the listener thinks of when he/she hears the piece.	There are highly effective examples of what the listener thinks of when he/she hears the piece.
Topic Sentence and Closing Sentence	The topic sentence does not introduce the piece and the closing sentence does not wrap up the description.	The topic sentence partially introduces the piece and the closing sentence is partially effective in how it wraps up the description.	The topic sentence introduces the piece and the closing sentence wraps up the description in a somewhat creative way.	The topic sentence clearly introduces the piece and the closing sentence successfully wraps up the description in a creative way.
Grammar	There are many grammatical errors.	There are frequent grammatical errors.	There are fewer than 7 grammatical errors.	There are fewer than 5 grammatical errors.

Assessment

Criteria	Self-Assessment	Teacher-Assessment
Vocabulary Usage	Circle one: 1 2 3 4	Circle one: 1 2 3 4
Examples	Circle one: 1 2 3 4	Circle one: 1 2 3 4
Topic and Closing Sentence	Circle one: 1 2 3 4	Circle one: 1 2 3 4
Grammar	Circle one: 1 2 3 4	Circle one: 1 2 3 4

Student Comments: (Write at least one comment about your work.) _____

_____ Total_____ out of 16 points.

Teacher Comments:_____

_____ Total_____ out of 16 points.

Name(s): _____ Class: _____ Date: _____

Music Vocabulary Sentences

Inspired by: _____ *by:* _____

Listen to the music and write down 6 different vocabulary words you can use to describe it. Then write a sentence that describes the music for each vocabulary word.

1. Word: _____

_____

_____

2. Word: _____

_____

_____

3. Word: _____

_____

_____

4. Word: _____

_____

_____

5. Word: _____

_____

_____

6. Word: _____

_____

_____

Draw a picture to go with your sentences.

Name(s): _____ Class: _____ Date: _____

Rubric for Vocabulary Sentences

Write 6 sentences about the music using 6 different vocabulary words. Complete this rubric and hand it in to your teacher along with your sentences.

1. I/We used 6 vocabulary words in sentences.

      ☺   😐   ☹

   Great Job!   OK   Needs Work

2. I/We used all 6 vocabulary words correctly.

      ☺   😐   ☹

   Great Job!   OK   Needs Work

3. I/We used examples from the music to help me write my sentences.

      ☺   😐   ☹

   Great Job!   OK   Needs Work

Name(s): _____ Class: _____ Date: _____

Rubric for Vocabulary Sentences

Write 6 sentences about the music using 6 different vocabulary words. Complete this rubric and hand it in to your teacher along with your sentences.

1. I/We used 6 vocabulary words in sentences.

      ✓   ✓   ✓

   Great Job!   OK   Needs Work

2. I/We used all 6 vocabulary words correctly.

      ✓   ✓   ✓

   Great Job!   OK   Needs Work

3. I/We used examples from the music to help me write my sentences.

      ✓   ✓   ✓

   Great Job!   OK   Needs Work

Listening Vocabulary Test

1. Name the three ways to listen to music and give an example for each.

a. _____ - _____

b. _____ - _____

c. _____ - _____

2. Fill in the blanks

Word	Definition
Piano	
	Loud
	A sudden, loud note
Tempo	
Dynamics	
	High notes vs. Low notes
	Person who writes music
	Person who directs a musical group
Crescendo	
	Gradually get softer

3. Write down the 6 dynamic markings on the lines below from softest to loudest:

(1)_____ (2)_____ (3)_____ (4)_____ (5)_____ (6)_____

4. Vocabulary Usage – Listen to the excerpt, write down 3 vocabulary words that help describe the piece and then write a sentence or two explaining HOW the word describes the piece.

Inspired by: _____ by: _____

- WORD _____ - _____

_____

- WORD _____ - _____

_____

- WORD _____ - _____

_____

Interpretation Lessons

These lessons are ones that build off of students' active listening experiences. They are more involved and allow students to really use their developing listening skills in both the music and general classroom.

1. Music – More detailed lessons can be used to teach **musical concepts** such as musical form. See *Für Elise* lessons 1-3, starting on page 87, as an example of this.
2. General – Many of these lessons are designed to be used for student **interpretation** in either music class or in the general classroom using mostly language arts skills.

This is where **collaboration** can really be used to its full potential. The music teacher can introduce the music and the classroom teacher can take those experiences back to the classroom for interpretation. Interpretation can be something you do in music class but also in other classes as well, especially in language arts. The table on the following page shows some of the parallels between music and the language arts. There are many ways to integrate the language arts into the interpretation of music: poetry writing, story writing, letter writing, development of the parts of speech, etc. Share the lessons from this book with each other as well as the format of the lessons so that they can be adapted to different genres of music as well as different aspects of the curriculum. Use them and modify them according to your grade level, interests, needs and teaching style.

Time Line
From the introduction of a piece to sharing their interpretations of the music through one of these lessons, the time line looks like this:
1. Background Knowledge
2. Listening Experience
    - Setting Purposes
    - Guided Questions
    - Activities
3. Introduction to Interpretation Lesson
4. Students Do Project
5. Sharing of Project

Throughout the time line, students should listen to the piece repeatedly. The more they listen, the more they will hear.

Does every piece of music need to be understood and interpreted?
The answer is no. In fact, there is a good chance that much of the music you listen to with your students will not be fully understood, nor should it be. This may bring up other questions like: How can one understand music? or Should we understand music? Music is not all written to be interpreted. The important thing is that the music is getting students to think and use their skills as well as simply being enjoyed.

A different question that is important to touch upon in our situation as teachers is this: *Does every piece of music need to be understood and interpreted with words?* Again the answer is no. Many times you cannot even begin to put music into words. Music, after all, is another language that is said to transcend the literal world. You may find that students often struggle to find the right words to use as they respond to music. Even the most world renowned music critics have a hard time finding the definitive words to explain a piece of music.

Students will respond to music in many ways. The challenge is for you, the teacher, to allow students the flexibility to respond to and interpret the music in ways that are comfortable to them. Think of Howard Gardner's Multiple Intelligences. If your students want to move, let them move, if they want to draw, let them draw, as long as they first and foremost listen. With these experiences, the students can then branch off and write about what they thought, felt and experienced.

Active Listening ⇨ Respond Through Other Medium ⇨ Inspired Writing

Another thing to remember is that there are times when passively or responsively listening to music is all right. Although our focus here is active listening, it's important for students to understand all aspects of listening and the roles they play in their lives.

Parallels Between Music and the Language Arts

Parallel	Language Arts	Music
Follows what I call the "BME Rule"	Every good piece of writing has a Beginning, Middle and End regardless of the form. (paragraphs, narratives, reports, expositions, etc.)	Every good piece of music has a Beginning, Middle and End regardless of form. (sonata, rondo, ABA, etc.)
Elements of a story	All stories have certain elements: (plot, character, problem, solution, climax etc.)	Music has many of the same elements as a story.
Audience	All texts are written for a certain audience: (self, children, adults, producers, teacher, employer, general public, etc.)	All music is written for a certain audience: (self, young listeners, older listeners, royal courts, certain group of people, general public, etc.)
Purpose	All texts are written for a certain purpose: (self-satisfaction, assignment, to make money, movie script, etc.)	All music is written for a certain purpose: (self-satisfaction, commission, to make money, opera/play, etc.)
Imagery	Readers make a mental picture of what they are reading in order to help them understand the context. (picturing the house where the characters in the book live, picturing the action in the climax of a book or story).	Listeners will often make a mental picture of what they hear in order to fully take in the music. (These may be concrete or abstract images: imagery of the melodic lines, imagery of the places music takes the listener.)

The Lessons

These lessons have been grouped by writing format:

- Sentences and Paragraphs (page 67)
- Narratives (page 69)
- Recounts (page 72)
- Letters and Monologues (page 85)
- Poetry (page 100)
- Other Ideas (104)

Each set of lessons will begin with an overview. Detailed lesson plans then follow for some of the summarized ideas. These are meant to take you step by step through the **complete active listening experience**. They are good to use especially when starting out for they break things down very simply.

Modeling

Don't forget that modeling for students how to actively listen is important. For a review of ways to do this, turn back to "Modeling Good Active Listening Skills" on page 16.

National Standards – Music

The following standards **in bold print** are the ones that are used and developed through these lessons as well as through the whole process of actively listening to music.

1. Sing, alone and with others, a varied repertoire of music.
2. Perform on instruments, alone and with others, a varied repertoire of music.
3. Improvise melodies, variations, and accompaniments.
4. **Use musical vocabulary and language to analyze and describe music.**
5. Read and notate music.
6. Compose and arrange music within specified guidelines.
7. **Know and apply appropriate criteria to music and music performances.**
8. **Understand the relationships between music, history, culture and other disciplines.**

Note: Standards 2 and 3 are also met through the lesson starting on page 105, "Rhythm Settings."

Sentences and Paragraphs

~Overview~

Objective: To write sentences and/or paragraphs using music as inspiration

Suggested Music to be Used: ANYTHING These ideas have no limits!

Topic Sentences, Main Idea
Usually if you ask the students what they thought of a piece of music, they will say something in general like, "That sounded like water falling." These types of responses can be treated like main ideas to be made into topic sentences. After establishing these main ideas about the piece, the students can go on to make detail sentences about the piece, a nice closing and you have a great paragraph.

Stretching Sentences/Sentence Pyramid
Take a word or phrase that a student wrote about the music during the active listening activity (#2 or #3 on page 43) and, as a class, start stretching it into a simple sentence. For example, if the phrase, "bouncing ball" was picked, then the class would add onto it to make it a sentence: "Bouncing balls flew through the air." Then the class would add another word or phrase they had on their lists to make the sentence longer: "Blue bouncing balls flew through the air." The class should keep adding onto the sentence until you have a lonnnnng sentence: "Blue polka-dotted bouncing balls flew through the cold air, up to through clouds and into the sky." Have students draw the sentence, pick out the adjectives, nouns, verbs, etc. Use the sentence for the beginning of a story. Have students write it, draw it, act it out or tell it.

NOTE: When assigning a paragraph for students to write, you may find the reproducible on page 59 and the rubric on page 60 helpful.

Paragraph – Descriptive
After brainstorming some good adjectives that come from hearing the piece, the students then incorporate their ideas into a descriptive paragraph about the piece. Students may also use a drawing made during a drawing activity (#8 or #9 on page 44).

Paragraph – Senses
Have students use the senses paper (page 103) and write about how their five senses react to the music they experienced. Use this paper to help write a paragraph.

Paragraph – Persuasive
This paragraph allows the student to state an opinion about the piece and back it up with evidence. The opinion may tell why someone else should or should not listen to the piece of music. It could be about the overall mood of the piece which may be backed up by an explanation of the melody and how it made him/her feel. Any opinion will do. This is also a great venue for using music vocabulary words.

Paragraph – Music Review
This paragraph simply allows the students to write a music review on the piece such as that which would be found in a magazine. It is a good way for students to practice their music vocabulary words. Use this idea in your music center or extend it so that students can write

actual reviews for the classroom newsletter or school newspaper or magazine. Have students who are interested in digital media use the idea of a music review to put together a mock radio show or a pod cast to play on the school web site.

Paragraph – Factual
This paragraph may tell about a piece's background, composer or about the things that can be heard in the piece – a sort of musical study. Again this is a great way for students to use their music vocabulary words. Use this type of paragraph to inspire some research where students can discover the historical significance of the piece's background.

Paragraph – Comparison
This type of paragraph may compare:
- Two pieces by the same composer
- The same piece performed by different artists
- The music of two different composers – (This is good to do after you have listened to a couple of pieces by different composers.)
- The music of two different genres

After spending some time on one of the things you will compare, decide on six key words that correspond. When you have lists for two or more things to compare, let students use these to help plan and write their paragraphs.

~Overview~

Objective: To write a narrative using music as inspiration

Suggested Music to be Used: *Sabre Dance* by Aram Khachaturian, any program music: music that attempts to paint a picture, describe and action or tell a story without any words and is usually accompanied by descriptive title. (You can use many other pieces of music to accomplish the same goal.)

Writing Narratives Many pieces of music tell a story. You can find elements of character, setting and plot in the piece. Students, with modeling, are able to listen for these elements in the music and transfer them into a story. Students can use graphic organizers or basic narrative plans to help them get their ideas down before writing their narratives. Examples of these can be found on pages 70-71.

During the listening experience, students should close their eyes and pretend they are walking around in the music while it is playing. Tell them to use all their senses to experience the music. Since the objective of this lesson is to come up with a story idea, your students will need to be guided in their discovery of setting, main character, problem, events, and solution. Simply asking them to find these story elements helps them to do just that.

- Where in the music is the beginning, middle and end of the narrative?
- What kinds of things do you see when the music is playing?
- Is there a person or animal in the narrative that is the main character?
- Where does the narrative take place?   What in the music told you that?
- What is the problem in the narrative?   What in the music told you that?
- What is the solution in the narrative?   What in the music told you that?
- What kinds of things happen to the main character before his problem is solved?

After your students have listened to the piece a couple of times, allow them to get some of their ideas down on paper. Instead of having them write it with words first, let them draw it. Students come up with fantastic drawings that resemble the story within the music. Have them draw a storyboard (page 71) or a 4-panel cartoon (page 49). A complete lesson for this is on page 47. From there, your students can tell the story orally or write it down. A graphic organizer, like the one on page 70, may also be helpful. Be sure to allow time for sharing!

For a lesson outline on how to plan for and teach musical narratives see the lessons for "Planning and Writing a Recount" starting on page 73. Although meant for a recount, many of the same concepts apply concerning how to get your students familiar with the music and how to go about getting their inspired ideas down on paper.

Name: _____ Class: _____ Date: _____

Inspired by: _____ *by:* _____

Character(s): _____

Setting: _____

Beginning: _____

_____

Problem: _____

_____

Details: _____

_____

_____

Solution: _____

_____

Making a Storyboard– Write or draw the parts of your storyboard in the boxes. Cut out the strips and paste them together to make one long strip of paper. You can roll the paper and insert it into a film canister for storage.

Name: _____

Date: _____

Inspired by: _____

by: _____

Setting	Main Character	Problem

Detail	Detail	Solution

~Overview~

Objective: To write a recount using music as inspiration

Suggested Music to be Used: Excerpts from Beethoven's *Pastoral Symphony*, other symphonic music from great composers, music from the Baroque time period, the toccata section of Bach's *Toccata and Fugue in d minor*, Big Band instrumental music, *In the Hall of the Mountain King* by Edvard Grieg.

You will find that even though a recount is different from a narrative, many of the same pieces of music can be used for both. It all depends on what your students hear when they listen as well as the types of guided questions you ask. At time students will imagine the character getting into a problem (narrative); at other times they may only see a sequence of events (recount).

Musical Recounts (AKA Sequence of Events) Oftentimes music doesn't necessarily tell a story with a conflict and resolution, but it can describe events that are happening. Students can use the various reproducible plans to get their ideas down before writing their events in a paragraph or story form.

Before listening to a piece you choose for a recount, make sure students understand what a recount is. It is a story with no pivotal problem or solution. Instead, it is a sequence of events, like the many books about Little Critter by Mercer Mayer. They tell stories of what happens to LC on various days, but there are no significant conflicts to resolve. Using excerpts from Beethoven's *Pastoral Symphony* works well because it is music that describes different scenes of the countryside. Using an excerpt is key, since you do not want to overwhelm your students with a long piece of music.

During the listening experience, students should close their eyes and pretend they are walking around in the music while it is playing. Tell them to use all their senses to experience the music. Since the objective of this lesson is to come up with a sequence of events, your students will need to be guided in their discovery of their setting, main character or characters, and events. Simply asking them to find these story elements helps them to do just that.

- Where in the music is the beginning, middle and end of the story?
- What kinds of things do you see when the music is playing?
- Who or what are the characters in the recount? What in the music told you that?
- Where does the recount take place?   What in the music told you that?
- When does the recount take place?   What in the music told you that?
- What is happening in the recount?   What in the music told you that?
- What are the different events in the recount?   What in the music told you that?
- Why is this recount happening?   What in the music told you that?

After you have allowed your students to listen to the piece a couple of times, you should allow them time to get some of their ideas down on paper. Instead of having them write it with words first, let them draw it. Students can use a 4-panel cartoon (page 49), the sequence of events paper (page 78) or a film strip (page 79) to draw their ideas of what is going on in the music. From there, your students can tell the story orally or write it down. Graphic organizers, such as the ones found on pages 80 - 84 may also be helpful. A detailed lesson plan for writing a recount can be found starting on page 73. Be sure to allow time for sharing!

Planning and Writing a Recount

Summary: A recount is a simple retelling of events that occur. Other names for this may be a sequence of events, retelling, news report or experience story. It is not a story where the main character has a problem that needs to be solved.

The basic format of a recount: the 5 W's (who, what, where, when, why) that set the scene and the events in sequential order.

Overall Objectives:
STUDENTS WILL:
- Familiarize themselves with music and how it can represent a recount.
- Utilize a plan for their recounts.
- Write their recounts using the proper form.

Curriculum Devise Used: recount, graphic organizers

Other Art Mediums Used: visual art, drama, movement

Background Knowledge: Students should be familiar with what a recount is and what it entails: who, what, where, when, why, and events in sequential order

Example Recount:
A day in the life of a dog.
A dance with lots of people.
Taking a walk in the woods.
(Musical recounts can be a good way to get students to listen for and provide more details to put in their stories.)

Literature Connection:
Read an example book that is written in recount form like the many books about Little Critter by Mercer Meyer. For example: *Just Shopping with Mom, Just Me and My Little Sister* and *Just Grandpa and Me*. (Wisconsin: Western Publishing Company, Inc.)

Lesson 1 – Familiarization with Piece

Lesson Summary: Familiarization with piece and how it can represent a recount
Time: 20 minutes
Objective:
STUDENTS WILL: Familiarize themselves with music and how it can represent a recount.

Layout of Classroom:
Whole class setting, ready to listen.

Materials and Preparation:

Teacher	Student
Recording of music	None
Picture of composer

Procedures:
1. Taking an active listening stance, play the piece once.
2. Get students' first reactions to the piece. The purpose for the next listening: Explain that they will be trying to picture the setting of the music and what is going on keeping in mind the 5 W's. They may want to close their eyes.
3. Taking an active listening stance, play the piece once again.
4. Get some students to tell what kinds of things were going on in the recount.
5. Taking an active listening stance, play the piece one last time.
6. Talk about where you hear the beginning, middle and end of the recount.
7. Discuss in detail where you believe the events are taking place (setting), when the events are, who is involved and basically what is happening. Be sure to explain what in the music makes you think this.
8. While the music is playing, tell the students some of the events that you believe are happening as the music progresses.
   (You will need to model this the first time you plan and write a recount to music by "thinking out loud" as outlined on page 16.)
9. Always end your time of familiarization with the piece by taking an active listening stance and playing the piece once.

Open-Ended Questions:
- Where in the music is the beginning, middle and end of the story?
- What kinds of things do you see when the music is playing?
- Who or what are the characters in the recount?   What in the music told you that?
- Where does the recount take place?   What in the music told you that?
- When does the recount take place?   What in the music told you that?
- What is happening in the recount?   What in the music told you that?
- Why is this recount happening?   What in the music told you that?

Assessment Tool: Student checklist of participation

Evaluation:
- Were students participating in the listening?
- Were students participating in the discussions?

Note:
Again, you will need to take the time and model where you believe the evidence of a recount is in the piece, stopping the music when you get an idea about where the recount takes place, who the recount is about, etc. As students become familiar with the idea that musical recount and written recount have the same elements, they will be able to pick them out on their own.

Lesson 2 - Planning the Recount

Lesson Summary: Planning the recount using one of many recount plans.

Time: 40 minutes

Objectives:

STUDENTS WILL:

- Choose a planning devise/art form with which they are comfortable.
- Utilize the art form to plan their recount.

Layout of Classroom:

Whole class setting for instruction with flexibility to allow students to work on their own.

Materials and Preparation:

Teacher	Student
Recording of music	Depending on what you and your students choose to do, you will have to make your own list.

Procedures:

1. Taking an active listening stance, play the piece once.
2. Allow students to remember and retell some of the recounts they came up with from the previous listening time.
3. Explain that students will be taking their ideas further by telling their recounts in fun ways.

You, as teacher may want to have the students do all the same plan format at first to "walk" them through a complete process of writing a recount using music as inspiration. As students become more comfortable with this, you may want to have students choose a way to tell their recounts.

Here are the planning ideas:

- Cartoons – A 4-panel cartoon with captions and/or speech bubbles. (page 49)
- Sequence Strip – A 7-box visual representation of each event. (page 78)
- Film Strip – This is a step up from a sequence strip that allows students to package their events in a film cartridge. (page 79)
- Graphic Organizer – With this, students will write out the parts of their opening, closing and the events before they write it in story form. You may want to use this more familiar planning idea initially and offer students the chance to retell their recount in one of the other ways after filling in a graphic organizer. (pages 80-84)
- Drama with People – Students can get into groups and act out their recounts in drama format. (Be aware that students will have different recounts to tell. Each group of students will need to take turns being the director who tells the others his/her recount to act out. This could also be an extension to making a film strip.)
- Drama with Objects – Students can use objects or puppets that they find or make to act out their recounts.

- <u>Movement</u> – This is where one student acts out, dances or mimes his/her own recount.
- <u>Music</u> – Students may want to use some instruments to tell their recounts or use them to enhance their drama. They may choose to write a ballad (a lyrical piece of music that has many verses) that depicts their recount.

Allow time for students to present their recount plans.

Open-Ended Questions:
- What have you done to show the 5 W's and events of the recount?
- What would you do differently next time?
- What would you do the same way?

Assessment Tool: Student participation and plan format

Evaluation: Did students show evidence of all recount parts?

Lesson 3 – Writing the Recount

Lesson Summary: Writing the recount using the plan students have finished

Time: 20 minutes teacher instruction with time for students to finish their recounts on their own.

Objectives:
STUDENTS WILL:
- Utilize their plan in order to write their recount.
- Use appropriate writing guidelines set up by the teacher.

Layout of Classroom:
Whole class setting for instruction with space for students to write

Materials and Preparation:

<u>Teacher</u>	<u>Student</u>
Recording of music	Their plan or remembrance of it
	Materials for writing a recount

Procedures:
1. Taking an active listening stance, play the piece once.
2. Discuss with students how the music inspired them and how they interpreted the music into a recount. Share some stories.
3. Explain that students will now take their recount plans and start to write them down in story form on paper.
4. At this time, you will need to explain your expectations concerning rough drafts, peer conferencing, etc.

5. Periodically, throughout the time students are working on their written recounts, play the piece for them.
6. Once the recounts are in final copy format, be sure to have some sort of presentation where students can listen to the piece and read their recounts for the class.

Open-Ended Questions:

- Did you enjoy writing a recount from music? Why or why not?
- How did the plan help you to write the recount down on paper?
- How is a musical recount like a written recount?

Assessment Tool:

- recounts: rough drafts, final copies and all other materials used
- editing checklist

Evaluation:

- Did students show evidence of using the piece of music to derive their recount?
- Did students use their plans to help them?
- Did students write their recount according to the teacher's standards?

Taking it Further:

- Have students discuss how musical recounts are like written recounts.
- Have students compare the two using a Venn diagram or other visual representation.

Sequence of Events– Write or draw your sequence of events in the boxes. Cut out the strips and paste them together to make one long strip of paper.

1	2	3

Name: _____

Date: _____

Inspired by: _____

by: _____

4	5	6	7

Making a Filmstrip– Draw the action parts of your story in the boxes. Cut out the strips and paste them together to make one long strip of paper. You can roll the paper and insert it into a film canister for storage.

Name: _____

Date: _____

Inspired by:

by: _____

Name: _____ Class: _____ Date: _____

Inspired by: _____ by: _____

Recount
Setting the Scene

When: _____

Who: _____

What: _____

Where: _____

Why: _____

Write these parts into a good setting sentence for your recount:

_____

_____

_____

Name: _____

Class: _____ Date: _____

Inspired by: _____

by: _____

Recount
Events

Make a web of the events that happened.

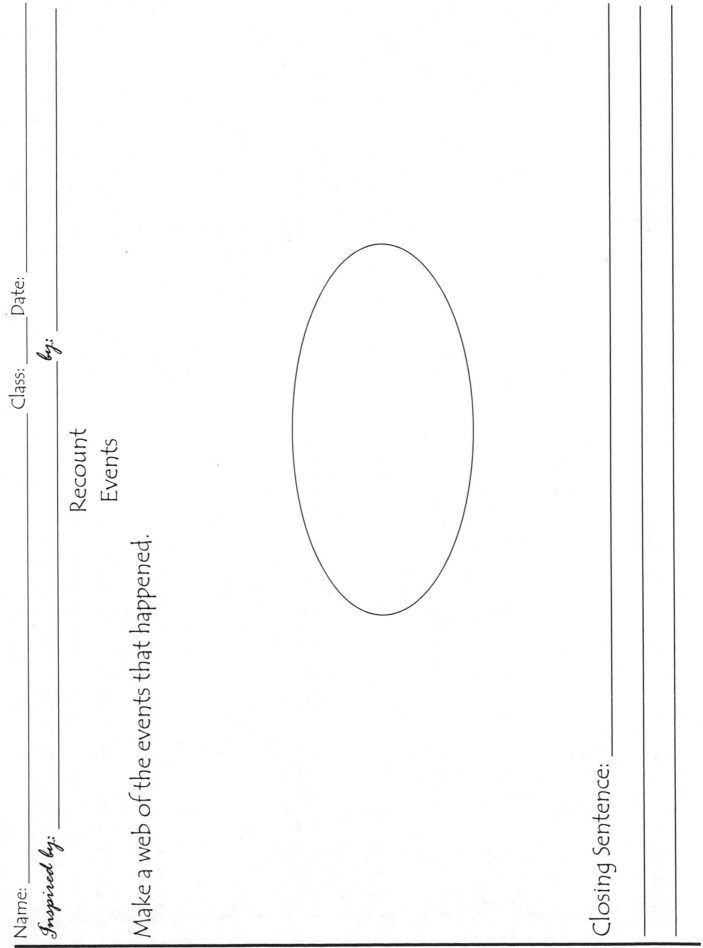

Closing Sentence: _____
_____
_____

Name: __Example__ Class: _____ Date: _____

Inspired by: __In the Hall of the Mountain King from Peer Gynt Suite No. 1__ *by:* __Edvard Grieg__

Recount

Setting the Scene

When: __Two years ago__

Who: __Sammy and Holly__

What: __went__

Where: __to the mountains__

Why: __to see if the mountain king was real__

Write these parts into a good setting sentence for your recount:

__Two years ago, Sammy and Holly went to the mountains to see if the mountain king was real.__

_____

_____

Name: _____ Example _____ Class: _____ Date: _____

Inspired by: _____ In the Hall of the Mountain King from Peer Gynt Suite No. 1 _____ *by:* _____ Edvard Grieg _____

Recount Events

Make a web of the events that happened.

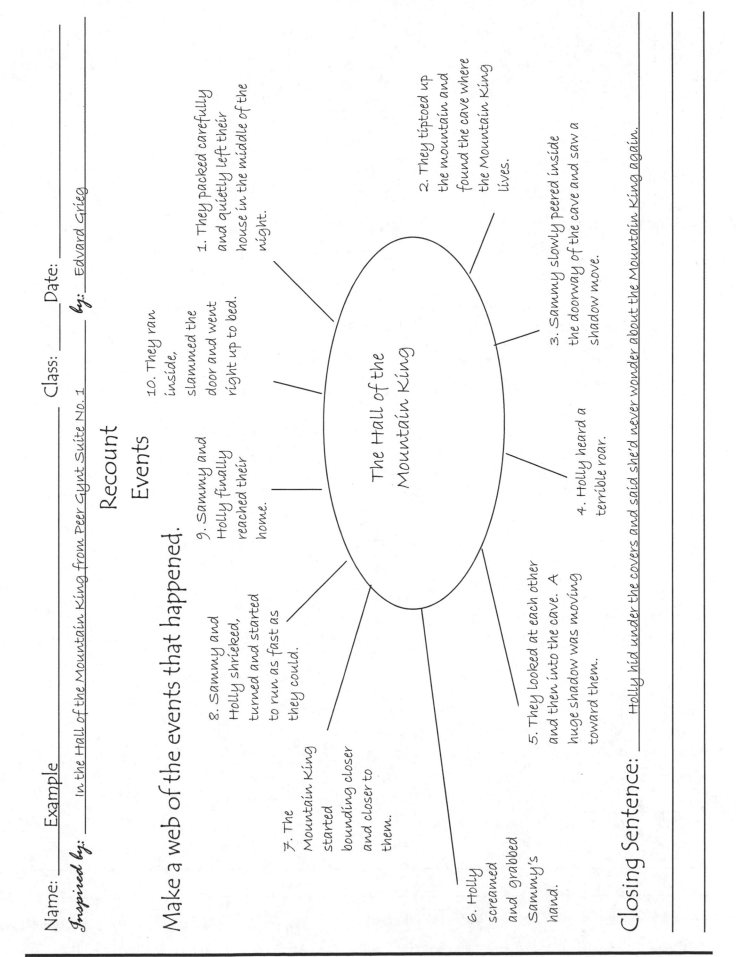

The Hall of the Mountain King

1. They packed carefully and quietly left their house in the middle of the night.

2. They tiptoed up the mountain and found the cave where the Mountain King lives.

3. Sammy slowly peered inside the doorway of the cave and saw a shadow move.

4. Holly heard a terrible roar.

5. They looked at each other and then into the cave. A huge shadow was moving toward them.

6. Holly screamed and grabbed Sammy's hand.

7. The Mountain King started bounding closer and closer to them.

8. Sammy and Holly shrieked, turned and started to run as fast as they could.

9. Sammy and Holly finally reached their home.

10. They ran inside, slammed the door and went right up to bed.

Closing Sentence: _____ Holly hid under the covers and said she'd never wonder about the Mountain King again. _____

Name: _____ Class: _____ Date: _____

Inspired by: _____ *by:* _____

Recount
Setting the Scene

When: _____

Who: _____

Where: _____

What: _____

Why: _____

Write these parts into a good setting sentence for your recount:

_____

_____

Events
Make a web of the events that happened.

Closing Sentence:

_____

_____

~Overview~

Objective: To write a letter or monologue using music as inspiration

Suggested Music to be Used:

- Any pieces that feature a solo instrument: *Für Elise* by Beethoven, piano; *Siciliano* by Vivaldi, violin; *Cliffs of Dover* by Eric Johnson, electric guitar; excerpts or movements from concertos
- Pieces that have a strong melody. Often you can think of it as if you are writing lyrics for the piece, although this doesn't mean the letter or monologue needs to be written like they ARE lyrics: *Pennsylvania 6-5000* by Glenn Miller

Musical Letters
Students write a letter using their interpretations of the music. The letter may be from the composer telling why he/she wrote the piece, from the audience about the piece, to or from an instrument in the piece, or it may have something to do with the background of the piece as in the *Für Elise* lessons that follow starting on page 87.

Musical Monologues
Students write a monologue using their interpretations of the music. The monologue can be written in the first person from the point of view of an instrument, the composer, the piece of music as a whole, the melody, the harmony, a theme within the piece or any other point of view.

The minor difference between writing a monologue and a letter is in considering the format with which you will write and the audience for whom you will write. In a monologue, you seem to be talking to no one in particular. You may want to think of it as talking to yourself in your head or as if you are reading a page in a diary. In a letter, you are writing to a particular person for a particular reason. At times, it may be necessary to know the background of a piece (such as for *Für Elise*), though, it is not always necessary.

Before listening to a piece of music for a letter or monologue, draw the students' attention to finding the mood of the piece or listening for a certain instrument or strong melody that will be the "speaker" or the main character. This abstract thinking may need to be modeled throughout the second listening. (The first should be uninterrupted enjoyment, followed by first impressions.)

As with the other types of writings, you may need to help students along with what they hear by asking them guiding questions.

Letter:
- Who do you believe the letter is from?
- How do they feel? Why?
- Who do you believe the letter is to?
- Why will this letter be sent?
- What do you think is being said in the letter? Why?

Monologue:
- Who do you believe is speaking in the monologue?
- How do they feel? Why?
- What are they saying?
- Why are they saying it?

After your students have had time to listen to a piece a couple times, you should allow them to get some of their ideas down on paper. The reproducibles are on pages 96-99.

The following set of lessons use the popular and familiar piece, *Für Elise* by Beethoven. In preparation for the interpretation part, students do some active listening activities that help them find the rondo form. This is a great set of lessons for both music class and language arts. I have used the same lessons for 2nd, 5th and 7th grade classes (music and general education) with success.

Outline of lessons for *Für Elise*:
Lesson 1 – Familiarization with Piece
     Listen for the first time
     Activity – Words and Phrases
     Activity – Musical Doodles
Lesson 2 – Discovering Rondo Form – Music Focus
     Listen to piece
     Compare two papers done for activities
     Discover rondo form through the activity papers
Lesson 3 – Interpretation: Writing the Letter – Language Arts Focus
     Explain background of piece (if haven't already)
     Listen to piece
     Introduce project – writing the letter
     Students work
     Share

Some example letters and monologues written by students of various ages can be found on pages 94 and 95.

Für Elise Letters

Summary: Students will do different active listening activities to find the rondo form of *Für Elise* by Beethoven as well as interpret the music itself. They will then use this information as inspiration to write a letter in the first person from Beethoven to Elise using the piece as a basis for interpretation.

Background Knowledge:

Rondo form: The teacher needs to familiarize him/herself with the form of the piece: ABACA. In *Für Elise*, there is a main theme "A" that occurs three times. This is the familiar tune that we often hear on cell phones and children's toys. The "B" section is lighter, almost reminiscent of days gone by. The "A" section is heard again. Section "C" is heavy and angry. The piece ends with one last playing of the "A" section.

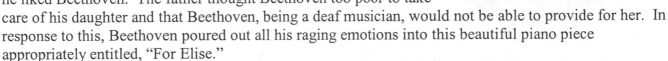

The story behind *Für Elise*: As the story goes, Beethoven had a pupil, Elise, whom he adored very much. However, when he went to her father to ask for her hand in marriage, her father refused even though he liked Beethoven. The father thought Beethoven too poor to take care of his daughter and that Beethoven, being a deaf musician, would not be able to provide for her. In response to this, Beethoven poured out all his raging emotions into this beautiful piano piece appropriately entitled, "For Elise."

Suggested Piece to be Used: *Für Elise* by Ludwig van Beethoven

Musical Content: rondo form

Complimentary Standards: words, phrases, parts of speech, visual – doodles

Lesson 1 – Familiarization of Piece

Lesson Summary: Writing words and drawing doodles to interpret *Für Elise*

Time: 40 minutes

Objectives:

STUDENTS WILL:
- Identify and list appropriate adjectives, nouns, verbs, and/or adverbs according to the music they hear.
- Illustrate with doodles what they interpret as they actively listen to the piece.

Layout of Classroom: Students work independently at desks, tables or floor areas, whole class sharing.

Materials and Preparation:

Teacher

Recording of *Für Elise* by Beethoven

Student

Word/Doodle Boxes Paper page 92
      (2 copies for each student)
Pencil, marker

In order to use this lesson as part of the Beethoven letter preparation, the teacher needs to familiarize him/herself with the form of the piece: ABACA. Each time the section changes, you will instruct the students to move to the next box on the paper.

Procedures: (These procedures can be broken up into two mini-lessons, if desired.)

1. In the first box of each paper, have students write: "*Für Elise* by Ludwig van Beethoven."
2. Taking an active listening stance, play and listen to the music.
3. Before playing the piece a second time, instruct students:

    "This time when we listen to the music, we are going to be writing words on the Word Boxes paper starting in Box 1. Write whatever words come to mind as you listen to the piece (nouns, verbs, adjectives, adverbs). Periodically throughout the piece, I will tell you to go on to the next box. So for example you will be listening to the music and you will be writing your words and then I will say 'Box 2.' Then you will begin to write words in Box 2 until I say 'Box 3.' We will listen to the piece two times."

    This is something you may need to model for your students. You may want to use a different piece (or an excerpt) or you can use an excerpt from this piece.

4. After playing the piece, allow time for students to discuss their words and tell why they put them down. Encourage students not to put down the words that others have said but to put down only words that they believe tell the true meaning of the piece. Share some of the words you put down.
5. Before playing the piece again, instruct students:

    "This next time, we are going to start in Box 1of your doodle papers. Periodically throughout the piece, I will stop the music and allow time for you to finish your doodles. When I start the music up again, go to the next box and begin a new doodle."

    This is also something you may need to model for your students using a different piece or excerpt.

6. After playing the piece once, allow them to go over their doodles again, this time without stopping the music. Instead, tell them when to go on to the next box.
7. Allow time for students to discuss their doodles and tell why they put them down.
8. Play the piece again and allow time for students to write down any other words or add to their doodles.

Open-Ended Questions:

- Are there many words that are similar or the same as what other students have? Are their any that are different? Why is that?
- Did you choose the words/doodles you did because you knew the story behind the piece? Discuss.
- How do the words/doodles in each box compare to one another?

Assessment Tool: Word Boxes and Doodle Boxes papers

Evaluation:
- There is no right or wrong answer.
- Content - Have the students completed the page with words?
- Effort - Have the students participated in the discussions?

Adaptations:
- Instead of words, write phrases or make short/long sentences.
- Start by writing a short sentence for a section and build on it in groups or as a class, adding phrases and words. (sentence pyramid, page 67)
- Instead of doodling in boxes, use adding machine rolls and make a continuous line of doodles.

Lesson 2 – Discovering Rondo Form

Lesson Summary: Using their interpretation guides (word/doodle papers), students will discover the form of the piece

Time: 30 minutes

Objectives:

STUDENTS WILL:
- Compare the Words Boxes and Doodle Boxes to find the musical patterns, thus discovering rondo form.
- Interpret each section of the piece in the point of view of the composer.

Layout of Classroom: Whole class setting with board, students will need desk space

Materials and Preparation:

<u>Teacher</u>

Recording of *Für Elise* by Beethoven

<u>Student</u>

Finished Word and Doodle Papers
Pencil, marker

Procedures:
1. Pass out the papers the students have completed thus far and have them display them on their desks so that both can be seen.
2. Taking an active listening stance, play and listen to the music while examining the pages.
3. Lead a discussion to help students find the patterns in the music that coincide with the papers.
4. As the discussion progresses, make the boxes on the board and write on them as necessary.
   Use different colors to represent the different sections.
   Use some of their words and doodle patterns to describe the sections.
5. See if students can now see how some of the boxes have similar words and/or doodles. (Some students will mention how the piece has a repeating part.)
6. Play the piece and every time the main theme ("A") is heard, ring a bell, have students clap or raise their hands, etc.
7. *Introduce the word THEME.*

8. Play the piece again and pause after the first theme is heard. Pointing to Box 1, say that what they heard was the section of music in Box 1, this is the *first theme*.
   "In music, we give a letter to each theme, so this would be called ... *Theme A*" Write "A" in Box 1 on the board, have students do the same.
9. Play the next theme, pause when it is done and point to Box 2.
   "That is the next theme. Was it the same or different from the first theme?" Different.
   "So, we will call it ... *Theme B*" Write B in Box 2 on the board, have students do the same.
10. Go through the piece until the boxes on the board and the students' papers are complete.
11. "Pull" out the letters, write them consecutively in the last box and call it RONDO FORM.
12. Have students do the same on their papers.
13. Listen to the piece one last time, pointing out and reinforcing the RONDO form.

Open-Ended Questions:
Discuss rondo form:
- Why did Beethoven use a reoccurring theme?
- Do we have reoccurring themes in the music we listen to today? (chorus, refrain) Why?

Assessment Tool: Word/Doodle Boxes papers with the theme letters written on them (ABACA).

Evaluation:
- Content - Have the students marked their pages to show rondo form?
- Effort - Have the students participated in the discussions?

Extension: Play another piece that follows the rondo form; have students identify the themes.

Lesson 3 – Interpretation: Writing the Letter

Lesson Summary: Students will begin writing the letter in the words of Beethoven using *Für Elise* as inspiration.

Time: 20 minutes teacher instruction with time for students to work on and finish letter

Objectives:
STUDENTS WILL:
- Interpret Beethoven's emotions as portrayed in the music.
- Create a letter in the first person from Beethoven to Elise.
- Show an understanding of the form and themes of the piece by providing evidence of them within the letter.

Layout of Classroom: Whole class setting with board, students will need desk space

Materials and Preparation:

Teacher	Student
Recording of *Für Elise* by Beethoven	Finished Word/Doodle Papers
Paper for rough copies of the letter	Pencil, marker
	Musical Letters paper (page 93) for final copy

Procedures:

1. Pass out the interpretation pages the students have completed thus far and have them display them on their desks so that both can be seen.
2. Taking an active listening stance, play and listen to the music while examining the pages.
3. Have a student reiterate the story behind *Für Elise*.
4. Listen to the piece again and in each box write down ideas about how Beethoven felt when he wrote the piece.
5. Explain that they will become Beethoven and put *Für Elise* into words, the words that Beethoven would've written had he composed a letter instead of music. They are to look at the Word/Doodle Papers in front of them and interpret each box into how Beethoven was feeling.

   Example: If a student believes Beethoven was feeling happy, he/she should say so in the letter (first person) and give evidence of it. See the student examples on pages 94 and 95.
6. Support your students as you see fit.

Open-Ended Questions:

- What have you learned about Beethoven?
- What have you learned about Elise and her father?
- What can you do with music that you can/can't do with words?
- What can you do with words that you can/can't do with music?

Assessment Tool:

- Interpretation pages with Beethoven's emotions
- Letter

Evaluation:

- Have students written down some of Beethoven's emotions in each box?

Letter:
- Has all necessary parts of a letter
- Has a date (1810)
- Is written in the first person
- Shows evidence of all themes
- Has correct grammar and punctuation
- Has good opening and closing statements
- Has a signature at the end

Adaptation: Write the letter as a class or in groups rather than each student writing an individual letter.

Extension: Write a letter as Elise or her father in response to Beethoven's letter.

Be sure to SHARE!

Name: _____

Class: _____

Date: _____

Word Boxes/Doodle Boxes

Inspired by: _____ by: _____	1	2	3	4
5	6	7	8	9

Name: _____ Class: _____ Date: _____

Musical Letter

Inspired by: _____ *by:* _____

_____

_____

_____

_____

_____

_____

_____

_____

_____

_____

_____

_____

_____

_____

_____

_____

Examples!

Here are some examples of word and doodle papers:

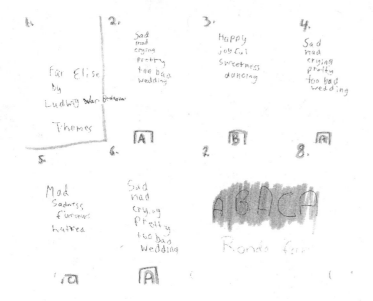

Here are some example letters written by students:

November 30, 1810

My Sweet Elise,

     I adore you so much. It would be so nice to be with you. I really want to marry you. You are so beautiful. I truly love you with all my heart. I hope you say yes my darling. I can't believe that your father said no. That was very selfish of him. I will do anything. I really think everything will be all right. I am very happy that I met you. You have lovely eyes. Oh please, oh please! I hope you write back. You are really sweet. Do not forget I love you.

         Your love,
         Beethoven

by a second grade boy

December 15, 1810

Dearest Elise,

There are so many things I want to say, but I have to fit them in this letter because I know I will never see your beautiful face again. We had so many good times together. We went dancing and to parties. It breaks my heart knowing I will never be loved the way you loved me ever again. In my head the words will stay, "You can't marry my daughter." I feel empty inside like I have no purpose on this earth. Please go off and find a richer, more handsome husband. You deserve better than me. I miss you already. What I would pay to spend one last day with you.

Your love forever,
Ludwig

January 7, 1810

Dear Elise,

I love you very much. My life was perfectly normal and life could not have been better. Then we decided to get married and I felt greater than ever. But your father turned me down and my heart was broken. I couldn't stop thinking of you. I was so sad. Then I was angry. The best thing in my life was you. Nothing good ever happened in my life! Then, I told myself that life goes on and it's not the end of the world. But I am still very sad.

Sincerely,
Ludwig

by a fifth grade boy

This is an example monologue written by a student using *Siciliano* by Vivaldi:

Try using one of the following four pages as a final copy of a monologue where an instrument is speaking. Have students place lined paper underneath to create an area where they can write on straight lines.

Master

My master's sister just died. I am sad, because my nightingale voice does not cheer him up, even though he tries to play me. He even asked other people to play beside him in case he breaks down. I hope he can feel better. He is the closest thing to me, besides my bow.

Inspired by: _____

by: _____

Name: _____ Class: _____ Date: _____

Name: _____ Class: _____ Date: _____

Inspired by: _____

by: _____

Name: _____ Class: _____ Date: _____

Inspired by Listening

Name: _____ Class: _____ Date: _____

~Overview~

Objective: To write a poetry using music as inspiration

Suggested Music to be Used: ANYTHING works with this!

Inspired Poetry
Some students like this type of poetry best. This is where students are free to write what they feel after listening to a piece of music. This poetry (as with many other forms) does not have to have a rhythm or rhyming scheme. You may opt to focus students who need a little more direction by having them do a words activity (#2 or #3, page 43). Once they have words down, they can pick a few words and/or phrases to help them write a poem. After students actively listen to two different pieces (and do the words activity for each), have them choose which piece they would like to use in a poem. I use this idea when my music students study Chopin, the "Poet of the Piano." We listen to *Waltz No. 1, Op. 64 No. 1 in D flat Major* and *Prelude Op. 28, No. 16 in b flat minor*. Then they choose one brainstorm of words to make into a poem that is inspired by the music. One example is on page 101.

Dada Poetry
Have students brainstorm words as they listen to a piece of music: 10 adjectives, 12 nouns, 10 verbs (or whatever you specify). Write words on cards: one word to a card or use the reproducible on page __. Put cards into a bucket and have students pick out 12-16 words. Students need to arrange the cards in an order that sounds good to them. Share the poetry.

This is also good to use with pieces with words. Write all lyrics on cards: one word to a card. Put cards into a bucket and have students pick out 12-16 words. Students need to arrange the cards in an order that sounds good to them. Share the poetry.

Parts of Speech Poetry
Pass out paper and have students write four words that come to mind as they listen to the music, one on each line: adjective, verb+ing, adjective, verb+ing. Next to each word, they need to write a phrase that goes with and will finish each line. Share the poetry. An example is on page 101.

Have students use words that are inspired by the music they hear in this format:
Line 1: Noun
Line 2: Adjective, Adjective, Adjective
Line 3: Verb+ing, Verb+ing, Verb+ing
Line 4: Adjective, Adjective, Adjective
Line 5: Noun (synonym to the noun in line 1)

Senses Poetry
Explain that when the students hear the music, they are to pretend to be "in" the music. (For example they are to throw themselves into the music.) While "in" the music they should use all their senses to experience the music. Give them a chance to find a comfortable position at their seats or

sitting on the floor. They may want to close their eyes for this. When they have done this, pass out the senses paper (page 103) and allow time for them to write down what they experienced in words or sentences. They may want to draw a picture beside each explanation. Give students time to circle some good words and phrases that they may want to use in their poetry. They can write these on a separate piece of paper (or papers) and make them into poetry. (Dada poetry works great with this too.) Students should share their poetry.

This concept of being "in" the music is very abstract and some students may have a difficult time with this. You can practice this skill by showing them a large poster of a piece of artwork. Have them throw themselves the piece of artwork and describe what they see, feel, taste, smell and hear while "in" there. Oftentimes, using a visual piece of art makes this concept a little easier to grasp.

Example Poems

This is an example of a "Parts of Speech Poem." It was written by a 5th grader and was inspired by *The William Tell Overture* by Rossini.

QUICK notes build the excitement,
GALLOPING across time.
STRONG bursts of sound,
EXPLODING through my ears like fireworks.

This "Inspired Poem" was written by a 7th grader. It was inspired by a short, exciting prelude by Chopin: *Prelude Op. 28, No. 16 in b flat minor.*

Rain

Yelling
Screaming
Loud
Dark Clouds
Rain,
Life is hard to maintain
When you're alone
Dancing in the rain
Sadness
Madness
Rain,
The pain
It's irresistible

DADA Poetry

DADA Poetry

Name: _____ Class: _____ Date: _____

My Five Senses

Inspired by: _____ *by:* _____

This is what I hear: _____

_____

_____

This is what I see: _____

_____

_____

This is what I feel: _____

_____

_____

This is what I smell: _____

_____

_____

This is what I taste: _____

_____

_____

~Overview~

The following lesson ideas can also be used in your classroom:

Musical Dialogues
Students write a dialogue using their interpretations of the music. This dialogue should be written with appropriate use of quotation marks. The dialogue can be between two instruments in a piece, two groups of instruments in a piece, between the melody and the harmony, between the composer and his piece, between the composer and another talking about the piece, between the student and any one of these.

This is also a great way to teach question and answer phrases in music. A question phrase is a short section of a melody (usually 2-4 measures) that ends on a high pitch just as our voice pitch does when we ask a question. An answer phrase almost always follows a question phrase and just as a vocal answer ends with a lower, definitive pitch, a musical one does the same. A good example of question and answer phrases can be found in Chopin's *Waltz No. 1 Op. 18 in E flat Major*.

Rhythm Settings
After students explore different rhythm instruments, they practice performing as a class or with a small group of students. These groups may perform for each other. Students actively listen to their own group or others and draw inspired images from them in order to create a setting for a story. Share and discuss. This can also be done with recorded music. Use a heavily rhythmic or other instrumental piece of music. A complete lesson for finding rhythm settings begins on page 105.

Character Profile
Students imagine the type of character that is created from the piece. The character may be "heard" in a single instrument or instruments or in the overall piece. They think about its personality, likes and dislikes, etc. Have students fill in the character profile sheet (page110) to gather ideas. They may write about the character and/or put the character into a narrative story. Students can make sock puppets or dolls using detergent bottle for their characters.

Rhythm Settings

Overall Objectives:
STUDENTS WILL:
- Explore different rhythm instruments and rhythms.
- Improvise and perform with the class in a drumming circle.
- Actively listen to the group perform.
- Draw images from the listening experience in order to create a setting for a story.

Musical Device Used: rhythm and rhythm instruments
(This lesson may also be done using an instrumental piece of music. Have students actively listen to the recorded music to get the idea of a setting instead of listen to the class performing. Example piece: *Rite of Spring* by Stravinsky)

Curriculum Device Used: narratives: setting
Other Art Mediums Used: visual art: drawing, painting, etc.

Part 1 – Playing Rhythms in a Group

Summary: Familiarization with rhythm and rhythm instruments

Time: 45 minutes

Objectives:
STUDENTS WILL:
- Explore different rhythm instruments and rhythms.
- Improvise and perform with the class in a drumming circle.
- Actively listen to the group perform.

Layout of Classroom:
Whole class setting. Rug area is preferred over desk/table space.

Materials and Preparation:

Teacher	Student
"Rhythm is Everywhere" papers (page 109)	Pencil
Place where students can fill out their papers (cafeteria, playground, classroom, hallway)	
Rhythm instruments (maracas, small drums, finger cymbals, etc.)	

Procedures:

1. Discuss what rhythm is and where it can be found.
2. Go to a place where students can actively listen to different rhythms they hear around them.
3. Give students 1-3 minutes of silence so that they can fill out their papers. (This also could be done as a **homework assignment** in preparation for this lesson.)
4. Share answers (Examples: people walking, talking, sway of branches, hum of computer, clock ticking) and discuss.
5. Pass out instruments and allow students 5-10 minutes of exploration playing. (You may want to devise some sort of system for students to try out a few instruments.)
6. Once students have one instrument each, give students time to practice and get acquainted with their instrument.
7. In a circle, one by one allow students to improvise on their own, showing the rest of the class the types of sounds the instrument can make.
8. Conduct a class drumming circle where the whole class plays together. This involves playing improvisation (making it up as you go) and listening at the same time which can be challenging, but not impossible. Explain to students that once they find a groove, they may want to close their eyes to help them listen as the class plays.

Hints for Drumming Circles

Don't be afraid to have a drumming circle in your classroom! They are fun; yes, loud, but fun. Do it at a time or in a place where you will disturb the fewest people and ALWAYS invite your fellow teachers and administrators to join in the fun! Here are some hints on how to conduct a casual, yet productive drumming circle.

- Start the rhythm with an **ostinato**. An ostinato is a simple rhythm that is repeated from the beginning to the end of the piece. You can play the ostinato or you can have a student or small group of students play one.
- Count the group in by saying, "One, two, three, four," and then start playing.
- To end the performance you can count them out, "One, two, three, stop!" Or you can let the piece end on it's own. Sometimes the piece will just end when the time is right.
- Encourage the students to **improvise** or make it up as they go. This is done by first listening to what others are playing and seeing how you can add to the piece by playing your instrument.
- Challenge students to look around at their classmates as they play. They can make eye contact with the people in the circle or watch the instruments they play. This is a way to communicate with others as you play.
- Introduce the word **groove** to your students and encourage them to find it. When a group can get into a groove with one another, then the real music begins to happen!

Open-Ended Questions:

- Was it easy or difficult to play with other people?
- Who felt comfortable? Who didn't? Why?
- After a while of playing together, did it get easier?

Assessment Tool: Student checklist

Evaluation: Were students participating?

Adaptations:
Have students perform for the class in smaller groups:
- Model a group performance:
    Pick 3 students to perform with you in front of the class. One by one each member of the group starts playing. You start, then a member joins you, then another, and then the last. Play for about a minute and end when the mood feels right.
- Divide students into groups of 3-5 and let them try their own group performances. They can perform on the spot for the class or you can allow time for groups to practice first before performing for the class.

Part 2 – Listening and Finding a Setting

Summary: Finding a setting in the rhythms

Time: 30-40 minutes

Objectives:
STUDENTS WILL:
- Improvise and perform with the class in a drumming circle.
- Actively listen to the group perform.
- Draw images from the listening experience in order to create a setting for a story.

Layout of Classroom:
Whole class setting; rug area is preferred over desk/table space.

Materials and Preparation:

Teacher	Student
Rhythm instruments	Paper
Drawing/painting paper	Drawing/painting materials
(or recording of instrumental music)	

Procedures:
1. Gather the class into the drumming circle. Make sure students have all their materials ready: instrument in front of them, paper and drawing materials placed behind them.
2. Have some practice time so that the class can get back into the groove of playing together.
3. Practice performing and having students actively listen at the same time. This is challenging for some students. You may invite them to close their eyes so that they can listen more easily. Have them focus on the place they image; the setting.

---

4. Once the performance is done, have students quietly put down their instruments and start a sketch of the place they imagined.
5. Do other performances and sketches, if desired.
6. When done, give students time to share their ideas with the class and complete one of their sketches with details.
7. Explain that these finished drawings will help students write a narrative. (They may simply give the setting of the narrative or the whole story may be in front of them.)

Open-Ended Questions:
- Was it easy or difficult to play with other people?
- Who felt comfortable? Who didn't? Why?
- After a while of playing together, did it get easier?

Assessment Tools:
- Student checklist
- Completed drawings/explanation of setting

Evaluation:
- Were students participating?
- Completeness of drawings (possible rubric)

Adaptations:
- If you choose to have small groups perform for the class, follow these procedures:
    1. One by one ask groups to perform in front of the class (The rest of the students will be closing their eyes in order to actively listen to the group.)
    2. After each group, allow time for students to sketch the images that came to them when they listened. (They should sketch simple drawings for each group – about 2-3 minutes each.)
    3. After all the groups have been heard, discuss some of the images students had and share some sketches.
    4. Students should pick one sketch and complete it with details.
    5. Explain that these drawings will help students write a narrative. (They may simply give the setting of the narrative or the whole story may be in front of them.)
- Replace these procedures with a listening of a recorded piece of music. Have students close their eyes and actively listen. Then allow time for students to draw the images that came to them when they listened. Have them think of the place they imagine so as to draw a setting for a story.

Name: _____

Date: _____

Rhythm is Everywhere!

_____

_____

_____

_____

_____

_____

_____

_____

_____

_____

_____

_____

_____

_____

_____

_____

_____

_____

_____

Name: _____

Date: _____

Rhythm is Everywhere!

_____

_____

_____

_____

_____

_____

_____

_____

_____

_____

_____

_____

_____

_____

_____

_____

_____

_____

_____

Name: _____ Class: _____ Date: _____

Character Profile

Inspired by: _____ *by:* _____

Pretend you are the character you hear in the music and finish these sentences in the character's words.

My name is _____.

I am _____.

I like _____.

I dislike _____.

My favorite food is _____.

My favorite place to be is _____.

My best friend is _____.

My favorite thing to do is _____.

This is a picture of me!

Assessment

An assessment is important to perform no matter what the subject, project, or unit. There are different ways to look at assessment. Sometimes it is ongoing where you check in with your students from time to time throughout a unit or project. Other times assessment is done at the end of a project or unit. An example of this is the test that accompanies a unit on the Musical Genres found on pages 160-161.

Ongoing Assessment

Many of the rubrics in this book are meant to help students assess themselves not only when they complete an assignment, but also as they work towards completion. Showing them a rubric or explaining your expectations from the start is key in getting great results.

Aside from rubrics, you can check in with students in other ways to see if they are understanding the material you are teaching. Checklists for participation, self-evaluation, check-up quizzes, a running record of class discussions and student conferences are other ways to do this. Have an attendance sheet handy and make marks next to students' names as they contribute something of value to a class discussion. This gives you a quick reference to see who is "getting it" and who may need extra assistance. Student conferences do not have to be time consuming and elaborate. Just a simple chat with a student as your class walks into the room may be all you need to get a grasp on how the student is doing.

Final Assessment

If you are a music teacher you will want to follow up a unit involving active listening with an assessment. An example of one, including reproducibles, can be found beginning on page 112. This assessment is designed to assess not only students' ability to think intelligently about the music but it also integrates with other parts of the curriculum. You may want to collaborate with other teachers on this. Students could do the research part (of the composer) in library class, the reviews in language arts, and the publication in computer class. The more collaboration you have among teachers, the more your students will get out of the assignment.

The following assessment was originally written and used with the upper grades, however it is easily adaptable for lower grades as well. An example of how to adapt such an assessment is shown beginning on page 118.

Make a Performance Program

Background

Whenever a piece of music or a selection of pieces is performed in a concert, there is a program available. A musical program is made up of various sections. There are illustrations, program notes on the composers and pieces and sometimes a few reviews about the piece made by other composers, musicians or listeners.

Task

Imagine that you have been hired to design, create and publish a program for a one-piece concert. In the program, you will need to write a brief description of the piece of music that includes at least 6 musical terms learned, a brief biography of the composer, an illustration to accompany the piece of music, and a couple of reviews of the music. There will be a front cover, inside portion and a back cover.

Front Cover: The cover must have an illustration that represents the piece of music as well as a title for the performance.

Back Cover: The back cover should have at least 4 reviews from other performers, musicians or listeners. These reviews must be 1-3 sentences long. For example, a review for Beethoven's *Ninth Symphony* may read, "Never before has a conductor fully represented the true emotion behind this piece of work. The orchestra grabs you from the beginning note and carries you through an amazing ride right through to the end. *–Boston Herald*" These reviews are ones that you create (you make them up), but they must be relevant to the pieces and performance.

Inside: One section of the inside will contain a biography of the composer who wrote the piece you have chosen. This biography must include basic information, as well as some interesting facts about his/her life. You must also include relevant information about the composer and this piece of music. For example, where was the composer when he/she wrote this? Why did he/she write this? It is recommended that you use the composer worksheet to help you gather information about the composer of the piece you chose.

Inside: The other section of the inside will be a description of the piece of music itself. You must actively listen to the piece of music and write a short essay about it. Use the skills you have learned in class to help you. There must be at least 6 vocabulary words used correctly in this description. It is recommended that you use the active listening worksheet to help you gather information about the piece you chose.

Audience
The audience for this program is the listeners who will attend the concert.

Purpose
The purpose of this program is to give the listeners some background for the piece of music and get them excited to listen to the piece of music.

Procedure
1. Choose a piece.
2. Actively listen to the piece. This will require you to listen to the piece multiple times.
3. Start to sketch out an illustration that represents your piece.
4. Fill in the worksheet for your piece.
5. Fill in the worksheet for the composer of your piece.
6. Draft the piece description, composer biography, and reviewers' blurbs.
7. Check your rough drafts using the rubric and make changes as necessary.
8. Show your work to an impartial observer and ask for feedback.
9. Make necessary changes.
10. Create your final drafts including the illustration.
11. Fill in the self-assessment section of the rubric and turn in your work.

Note
You will have time in class to complete this project; however, you may need to do some of this on your own at home. Please plan accordingly and ask for help whenever you need it.

Due Date
The due date for this project is: _____

Your program will be

Inspired by: _____ by: _____

Name: _____ Class: _____ Date: _____

Composer Worksheet

Use this worksheet to help you come up with the facts you need for the composer biography section of your program.

Composer's full name: _____

Date and place of birth: _____

Date and place of death: _____

3 Interesting facts about this composer:

    1. _____

        _____

    2. _____

        _____

    3. _____

        _____

Relevant information about the composer and the piece he/she composed:

    Where was he/she when it was composed?

_____

    Why did he/she compose it?

_____

_____

    What was happening in the world when it was being composed?

_____

_____

    Was it composed for someone in particular? _____ Who? _____

    Was it composed for as specific purpose?_____ What? _____

_____

    Other interesting information:

_____

_____

Write down any other information about this composer you might want to add to your biography:

_____

_____

_____

_____

Name: _____ Class: _____ Date: _____

Active Listening Worksheet

Use this worksheet to help you come up with the information you need to write the description of the piece of music for your program.

Title of piece: _____
Date piece was composed:_____
Write a few notes about what this piece makes you think of when you listen to it.

_____
_____
_____
_____

Write down 6 vocabulary words you can use to help describe the piece of music. Also include how you can use these words in your description.

Vocabulary Word	How you can use it in your description: (where it is, what it reminds you of, how it effects you as a listener)

Write a topic sentence that clearly introduces the piece of music.

_____
_____

Write a closing sentence that will successfully and creatively wrap up your description. Leave the reader excited to listen to the piece of music.

_____
_____

Name: _____ Class: _____ Date: _____

Rubric for Performance Program

Use this rubric to help you do the best job you can do! When you are done with your first drafts, have someone read what you have and help you determine where you are in your progress. Make changes as necessary and then complete your final copy.

When you are done with your final copy, complete the self-assessment section of this rubric. Pass this in with your final copy.

Criteria	Level 1	Level 2	Level 3	Level 4
Front Cover	Illustration is not neat or complete. It is not in color. It is hard to tell if the illustration represents the piece of music.	Illustration is somewhat neat and complete. It is in color. Illustration somewhat represents the piece of music.	Illustration is neat, complete and in color. Illustration effectively represents the piece of music.	Illustration is neat, complete and in color. Illustration very effectively represents the piece of music and shows detail.
Back Cover	There are less than 4 reviews written. There are errors in the format. The reviews do not seem to be relevant to the piece of music.	There are 4 reviews written. There are some errors in the format. The reviews are partially thoughtful and creative. They seem to be generic and could apply to other pieces of music.	There are 4 complete reviews written in the correct format: ("", 1-3 sent., reviewers' IDs). The reviews are somewhat thoughtful and creative. They seem to be relevant to the piece of music.	There are 4 complete reviews written in the correct format: ("", 1-3 sent., reviewers' IDs). The reviews are thoughtful and creative. They are relevant to the piece of music.
Inside – Composer Biography	An introduction gives little to no basic information about the composer.	An introduction gives some of the basic information about the composer.	An introduction somewhat effectively gives the basic information about the composer.	An introduction effectively gives the basic information about the composer.
	There are no relevant or interesting facts given about the composer.	There are few relevant or interesting facts given about the composer.	There are some relevant and interesting facts given about the composer.	There are many relevant and interesting facts given about the composer.
	There is no relevant information about the relationship between the composer and the piece.	There is little relevant information about the relationship between the composer and the piece.	There is some relevant information about the relationship between the composer and the piece.	There is plenty of relevant and valuable information about the relationship between the composer and the piece.
	There are many grammatical errors.	There are frequent grammatical errors.	There are fewer than 7 grammatical errors.	There are fewer than 5 grammatical errors.

Inspired by Listening

Criteria (continued)	Level 1	Level 2	Level 3	Level 4
Inside – Description of Piece	Most of the vocab words are not used correctly or there is little evidence that the writer knows the meaning of the words.	3-5 vocab words are used somewhat correctly. Other vocab words are not used correctly or there is little evidence that the writer knows the meaning of the words.	At least 5 vocab words are used somewhat correctly.	All 6 vocab words are used correctly.
	There are ineffective examples of what the listener thinks of when they hear the piece or there are none.	There are moderately effective examples of what the listener thinks of when they hear the piece.	There are effective examples of what the listener thinks of when they hear the piece.	There are highly effective examples of what the listener thinks of when they hear the piece.
	The topic sentence does not introduce the piece and the closing sentence does not wrap up the description.	The topic sentence partially introduces the piece and the closing sentence is partially effective in how it wraps up the description.	The topic sentence introduces the piece and the closing sentence wraps up the description in a somewhat creative way.	The topic sentence clearly introduces the piece and the closing sentence successfully wraps up the description in a creative way.
	There are many grammatical errors.	There are frequent grammatical errors.	There are fewer than 7 grammatical errors.	There are fewer than 5 grammatical errors.

Assessment

Criteria	Self-Assessment	Teacher-Assessment
<u>Front Cover</u>	Circle one: 1 2 3 4	Circle one: 1 2 3 4
<u>Back Cover</u>	Circle one: 1 2 3 4	Circle one: 1 2 3 4
<u>Composer Biography</u> Introduction Interesting Facts Relationship to Piece Grammar	Circle one: 1 2 3 4 Circle one: 1 2 3 4 Circle one: 1 2 3 4 Circle one: 1 2 3 4	Circle one: 1 2 3 4 Circle one: 1 2 3 4 Circle one: 1 2 3 4 Circle one: 1 2 3 4
<u>Description of Piece</u> Vocabulary Examples Topic and Closing Sentence Grammar	Circle one: 1 2 3 4 Circle one: 1 2 3 4 Circle one: 1 2 3 4 Circle one: 1 2 3 4	Circle one: 1 2 3 4 Circle one: 1 2 3 4 Circle one: 1 2 3 4 Circle one: 1 2 3 4

Student Comments: (Write at least one comment about your work.)

_____

_____Total _____ out of 40 points.

Teacher Comments:

_____

_____Total _____ out of 40 points.

Make a Performance Program

Background
Whenever you go to a concert, you get a program that tells you things about the music you are about to hear. It is your job to make a program like this for one piece of music.

Task

Front Cover: Your front cover must have the title of the piece of music as well as the composer's name. Make an illustration that goes with what you imagine is happening in the music as you actively listen and put that on the cover as well.

Back Cover: On the back cover write 3 opinions about the piece of music. They can be opinions you have or opinions from your classmates.

Inside: On the inside of the program you must have information about the composer: name, date of birth, date of death, and at least 3 interesting facts.

Inside: In another section of the inside, you must have at least 3 sentences that describe the piece of music. You must use at least 3 vocabulary words correctly in your sentences.

Audience
You are creating this program for the listeners who will attend the concert.

Purpose
The purpose of this program is to give the listeners some background for the piece of music and get them excited to listen to the piece of music.

Procedure
1. Choose a piece.
2. Actively listen to the piece at least 3 times.
3. Start to sketch out an illustration that goes with what you imagine when you listen to your piece.
4. Fill in the worksheet for your piece.
5. Fill in the worksheet for the composer of your piece.
6. Check your work using the rubric and make changes.
7. Pass in your worksheets to get feedback on how you are doing.
8. Make necessary changes.
9. Create your final drafts including the illustration.

Note
You will have time to work on this in class; however, you will also need to do some work on this at home. Please plan ahead and ask for help whenever you need it.

Due Date
The due date for this project is: _____

Your program will be

Inspired by: _____ by: _____

Composer Worksheet

Use this worksheet to help you come up with the facts you need for the composer biography section of your program.

Composer's full name: _____

Date and place of birth: _____

Date and place of death: _____

3 Interesting facts about this composer: (Write these in complete sentences.)

1. _____
   _____
2. _____
   _____
3. _____
   _____

Draw a picture of the composer here. (You may want to include a drawing of your composer in your program.)

Name: _____ Class: _____ Date: _____

Active Listening Worksheet

Use this worksheet to help you come up with the information you need to write the description of the piece of music for your program.

Title of piece: _____

Date piece was composed: _____

Write a few words or phrases that come to mind when you listen to this piece.

_____

_____

_____

_____

Draw what comes to mind when you listen to this piece.

Write down 3 Vocabulary words you can use to help describe the piece of music. Also include how you can use these words in your description.

Vocab Word	How you can use it in your description: (where it is, what it reminds you of, how it effects you as a listener)

Name: _____ Class: _____ Date: _____

Rubric for Performance Program

Use this rubric to help you do the best job you can do!

Hand this to your teacher along with your final performance program.

1. My program has the title of the piece and the composer's name printed neatly on the front cover.

   Great Job!   OK   Needs Work

2. I made an illustration that goes with what I imagined while actively listening to the piece of music. I put it neatly on the front cover of the program.

   Great Job!   OK   Needs Work

3. I wrote 3 opinions about the piece and put them neatly on the back cover of the program.

   Great Job!   OK   Needs Work

4. The inside of my program has at least 3 interesting facts written about the composer. They are written neatly and in complete sentences.

   Great Job!   OK   Needs Work

5. The inside of my program has at least 3 complete sentences that describe the piece.

   Great Job!   OK   Needs Work

6. These 3 sentences use at least 3 vocabulary words correctly.

   Great Job!   OK   Needs Work

Student Reflection

It is important to allow students a chance to reflect on a unit or assignment even after the big test or project has been completed. This allows time for students to really think about the experiences in which they have been involved. There are different ways to do this: class discussions, personal communication with individual students, written reflection questions, and/or a portfolio.

Here are some sample reflection questions for different areas of the unit. These questions are not supposed to have set answers, each student may answer differently.

In General:
- What do you know now that you didn't know before?
- What are three things you learned from this unit or project?
- What was the most difficult part of this unit or project?
- What was the easiest part of this unit or project?
- If you were to do this unit or project again, what would you do differently?
- If you were to do this unit or project again, what would you do the same?
- What was the best part about this unit or project?

For the Vocabulary:
- What do these terms allow you to do?
- What do you do differently now that you could not do before?
- Have you seen or heard any of these words being used in other areas or subjects?
- In what ways can you use these terms outside of class?
- What other things would help you to speak intelligently about the music you listen to?

For the Listening Experiences:
- Do you listen differently now than you did before? Why?
- What is the most valuable way to listen to music?
- How does listening to music help you?
- Will you listen to music more, less or about the same in the future as you have in the past?

Questions to Accompany a Selection to be Placed in a Portfolio:
- What item did you choose to put in your Portfolio?
- Why?
- Was this something you did yourself or with others?
- Who helped you complete this?
- *Add some of the other "general" reflection questions for students to answer.*

PART THREE

BACKGROUND KNOWLEDGE

Learning Background Knowledge

Giving students a basic knowledge about the composer or genre of a piece is important. It allows them to see another level of the music. A student may begin to understand what relevance the music had to a composer's life (why the composer wrote the music he did), how events in history affected the sound of the music (evolution of instruments) or any number of other things. Students gain a sense about the music that makes the listening experience much more real to them. They find a connection with the music that is of a new dimension.

Knowing the **genre** of music they will be listening to, the **time frame** around it, the **composer** who wrote it and what was going on in the **world** can be beneficial to the students' active listening experience.

Example:

Music Used: *Symphony #3, Eroica* by Ludwig van Beethoven

Before listening, students should know a little bit about Beethoven and the circumstances surrounding this symphony. Here is a concise summary: Beethoven lived in the time of the French Revolution. He himself was a man who believed in the ideals that many revolutionaries did: those of freedom, equality and justice. One man that Beethoven admired was Napoleon, who early on strove to uplift the "common man." To revere him as a great general and person, Beethoven wrote his 3rd symphony naming it *Bonaparte* after him. However, after finding out that Napoleon proclaimed himself Emperor of France, Beethoven decided against it, believing that a man should not do such an audacious thing. He ripped up the title page, renamed the piece *Eroica*, the "Heroic" Symphony and decisively dedicated it, "to the memory of a great man."

After learning about the background of this piece, students should use the listening experience to hear how the music portrays heroism and other values implied during a revolution. Interpretation lessons can include letter writing from Beethoven to Napoleon or from Napoleon to Beethoven or a music review for a newspaper set back in 1804.

COMPOSERS

It is important for students to know the composers who wrote the pieces they listen to both in and out of the classroom. It allows them to find another dimension to the music and they begin to understand why some music sounds the way it does.

As we read and teach the lives of these composers and musicians to children, it is important to see that for all these people, music brought them what they needed. To some, that need was enjoyment and happiness, to some it was money, to some it was peace and to many it was how they expressed their feelings. It is necessary to point out that everyone has his/her own way of fulfilling personal needs. Some students might know that they like to write in a journal to get their feelings out, some may like to talk things out with other people. Others may turn to drawing and painting. Your students may find that music is what they connect to in order to sort out their own feelings.

Personal Parallels

The lives of many composers can parallel those of the students and by learning about their lives the students are more drawn to their music. For example, students feel compassion when they learn that Beethoven was an abused child or that Bach was an orphan. Baseball players love the fact that Gershwin would rather have played ball than touch a piano. Piano students like to hear that even Duke Ellington didn't always like to practice the piano when he was young. Often the students find a little bit of themselves in the composers and their music becomes more alive.

Pictures and Timelines

One way to get students familiar with the composers is to show them pictures. These pictures may be of the composers themselves or even sample artwork from the time period of the composer or piece. Using various pictures allows opportunities to talk about how art, architecture, fashion and style evolved over the centuries, just as the music did.

A great way to display the pictures of composers and artwork is on a timeline. This allows students to get a sense of time frames, to see how each composer may have influenced the next and to see how the music they listen to relates to historical events. For example, who was composing music during the Revolutionary War in America? Are there any connections between the two?

Books and Read-Alouds

There are so many good books about the lives of composers, about genres of music and about music in general. Old and new, in book stores and libraries, informational and biographical picture books - you name it, they're out there. Reading story books is an excellent way to introduce the life of a composer to your students. Students will also show an interest in revisiting those and other books made available to them. A list of books can be found in the resource section at the end of this book.

Extensions

As time goes by, students may show their own motivated interest to find more information. This information may come from other books; in magazines; CD, tape or record jackets; or the internet. You may want to collaborate with the librarian or computer teacher to encourage research skills. Students love knowing that these composers exist outside the classroom!

Sketches

Please note that the following biographical and informational sketches are just that: sketches that do not attempt to give the full life of any musician nor the full history of any genre. These are meant to give the teacher background knowledge in order to tell his/her students points of interest of a composer's life (especially how they began) or genre. These are the things that will hopefully whet students' interest to find out more for themselves.

Antonio Vivaldi (1678-1741) was born on March 4 in Venice, Italy. He is most wellknown for his association with his favorite instrument - the violin for which he became a virtuoso. At fifteen, Vivaldi decided to go into the priesthood and soon received a nickname, "*Il Prete Rosso*," literally, "the Red Priest" for his flaming red hair. Many times while celebrating mass, Vivaldi would stop and leave the altar complaining of chest pains. It is said that Vivaldi wasn't really soothing an ailment, but was writing down some inspired ideas for a melody before he forgot them. This is believable since these pains never occurred while he was directing an orchestra or playing the violin. While in his early twenties, Vivaldi found, what was for him, the perfect job at an orphanage for girls in Venice named *Ospedale della Pietà,* (Hospital of Mercy). There he was director, performer and teacher to many of the girls, some of whom would grow to become virtuosos themselves. Performances occurred on Sundays and on feast days, drawing large and appreciative audiences. Vivaldi also composed a great number of pieces while working at the orphanage. Rumor has it that Vivaldi would complain that his pen didn't write as fast as his mind could think of melodies. Vivaldi was a great man who bestowed an enormous gift on the children of Venice. His works, including *The Four Seasons,* are both brilliant and beautiful.

Johann Sebastian Bach(1685-1750) came from a long line of musicians. Of his 200 relatives, 193 of them were professional or amateur musicians. In Germany, after three solid centuries of musical Bachs, any musician was likely to be referred to as "a Bach." At the age of ten, young Bach's parents died and he was left in the care of his brother, Johann Christoph, an organist at the church at Ohrdruf. Johann Christoph was very jealous of his younger brother's talent; so much so that he wouldn't let him use his musical scores. Instead, he locked the music in a cabinet. At night, when his brother was sleeping, young Bach would turn the pages of the book through the lattice work of the doors, copying the music page by page by the light of the moon. This copying took six months and is said to have permanently damaged his eyes. He completely lost his eyesight by 1749, the year before he died. When his brother discovered what he had been doing, he took away the copies he had made, but that did no good because young Bach had memorized the music in the process of copying it!

After his brother died, Bach began singing with the choir of St. Michael's in Ohrdruf, and studied from their library of music. At nineteen years of age, Bach became the organist at Arnstadt. There he became so proficient in the work he did that he became known to musicians in other cities. In the years to follow, Bach was an organist in many churches and served as chief musician in courts of royalty, usually writing music for specific important occasions or functions. The last thirty years of his life were spent as music director of St. Thomas School at Leipzig. Bach had become so famous that no musician would pass through the city without making Bach's acquaintance or hearing him perform.

Bach was married, widowed and married again. He was the father of twenty children, all of whom were musicians. Bach's music includes that of keyboard, vocal and instrumental, though he is most famous for his organ works, the organ being his favorite instrument. His complete works fill 46 huge volumes and consist of several thousand compositions. Some of his most well-known compositions include his works for the *Well Tempered Clavier* which consists of 48 preludes and fugues in every key and the *Toccata and Fugue in d minor.*

George Frederic Handel (1685-1759) showed

a great interest in music at an early age, as he taught himself how to play the harpsichord, an early keyboard instrument. His father, however, did not want his son to become involved with music, wanting him instead to become a lawyer. It was only after the German Duke of SaxeWeissenfels heard young Handel play the organ that Handel's father gave in and allowed him to take music lessons beginning at the age of seven. By the age of 11, he was proficient in harpsichord, violin, and oboe and had become assistant organist to his teacher at Halle Cathedral.

Although Handel's father had died, his influence remained with Handel and in 1702, he enrolled in Halle University as a law student, but he kept his position as organist.

By 1710, Handel had become choirmaster to King George I of Great Britain and soon moved permanently to England. Handel composed numerous pieces of music including about fifty operas and numerous oratorios. Oratorios are religious words (usually from the Bible) which are set to music and sung by soloists and a choir. Handel's most famous piece of music, *Messiah*, is an oratorio. It is difficult to go through a holiday season without hearing the *Hallelujah* chorus from the *Messiah*. Another well-known piece of music from Handel is his *Water Music* which got its name when Handel and his musicians accompanied George I on a river boat ride performing in an adjacent boat.

Franz Joseph Haydn (1732-1809) was a great composer and teacher. Both Mozart and

Beethoven were among his students. He worked nearly thirty years for a Hungarian noble family, the Esterházys. There, Haydn was "head musician" which meant he was in charge of all things musical including repairing instruments, tending to rehearsals and, composing music for Prince Nicholas. Haydn composed music for dinners and dances, concerts and strolls in the garden. He was Prince Nicholas's personal I-Pod as he composed and performed all the music the prince demanded. One of his responsibilities was to oversee all the other musicians as well, and he did this with such care and compassion that they gave him the name "Papa Haydn." He was their father figure when they would be away from their families much of the year at Prince Nicolas's summer palace, Eszterháza, in the remote Hungarian countryside. Today, Haydn is known as "The Father of the Symphony," as in his lifetime he composed 104 symphonies, perfecting the form.

Wolfgang Amadeus Mozart (1756-1791) was born on January 27 in Salzburg, Austria. At

the age of three, young Mozart enjoyed sitting at the keyboard and picking out melodies that delighted him. By the time Wolfgang was four, his father Leopold, also a musician, would teach him simple pieces. Maria Anna, Mozart's sister, (they were the only surviving children of seven,) recalled many years later, "he learned a piece in an hour, and a minuet in half and hour, so that he could play it faultlessly and with the greatest delicacy, and keeping exactly in time. He made such progress that by the age of five he was already composing little pieces." It was no doubt that Mozart was a child prodigy. Leopold was excited by this discovery and, although he felt a bit guilty about it, he was eager to show off his son immediately in order to get the most financial benefit. He also was certain that Mozart's gifts were God-given and saw it his duty to share his son's talents. So, before Mozart's sixth birthday, Maria Anna and young Mozart set out touring much of Europe with their parents.

Mozart's ability to sight read any music put in front of him and to improvise at the keyboard greatly impressed his audiences. He truly enjoyed playing, performing, and of course, showing off a bit. He was a true genius of music, playing complex pieces of music after hearing the piece only once. Traveling through Europe for many years, Mozart played for church hierarchy and royalty and was commissioned to write for kings and emperors.

Mozart was a happy man, though he fell into financial difficulty as he and his wife, Constance Weber, lived a life well beyond their means. Composing for the public performances had become their main source of income so Mozart composed as much as he could during this time, including his three most famous operas: *Don Giovanni, The Magic Flute*, and *The Marriage of Figaro*.

Mozart died impoverished at the early age of 35 and was given a pauper's funeral, which unfortunately meant he was buried without a coffin in an unmarked grave. The legacy, however, that Mozart left behind will live forever and he will always be known as one of the greatest musicians of all time.

Ludwig van Beethoven (1770-1827) was born in Bonn, Germany on December 16. His childhood was full of troubles and unhappiness, mostly brought on by his cruel father Johann. His father, being his first teacher and seeing that he had talent, wanted Beethoven to be the next Mozart. In turn, Johann believed he would gain some recognition and financial benefit for himself. He suffered from a disease that had no name at the time: alcoholism. He was ill-tempered and often beat his son when his playing displeased him. Often, young Beethoven was awakened in the middle of the night to practice and if the sleepy, young boy played a wrong note, his ears were boxed or his knuckles were struck. When Beethoven was seven, Johann provided the opportunity for his young son to give his first public performance. When the performance was not a success, Johann yelled at Beethoven, believing him a failure and complaining that he would never become the next Mozart.

Beethoven then had a line of bad teachers who were mostly friends of his father and only taught him after they had spent much of the night at the tavern. Finally, Beethoven studied under Christian Gottlob Neefe, a fine new teacher who took Beethoven under his wing and taught him in an orderly and disciplined manner. Under his tutoring, Beethoven learned all of Bach's 48 Preludes and Fugues and organ works. As a result, Beethoven got his first paying job as court organist at fourteen years old.

After Neefe, Beethoven traveled to Vienna to audition for the opportunity to study with Mozart. Although his audition impressed Mozart, Beethoven was not able to study with him. His mother had grown sickly and soon died. Beethoven was needed at home and by the time Beethoven was able to return to Vienna, Mozart had died. Beethoven, however was taken on as a student of the great Franz Joseph Haydn. The teacher/student relationship was unique and although the two clashed in personality, they both respected each other greatly.

In 1796, at the age of 26, Beethoven started to lose his hearing. The process of his hearing loss was very slow and Beethoven often became depressed because of this. He could not understand why he, a composer, one who makes his living with music, would lose his sense of hearing. Nevertheless, he kept composing and amazing his audiences. Even at full deafness, though he had to quit working as a concert pianist, Beethoven continued to compose. He heard the music in his head, often on the many walks he would take through town, and would transfer the notes onto paper once he arrived back home. One such work is his *Ninth Symphony* – a musical milestone in itself, as it is the first symphony to use a full chorus and four soloists.

Beethoven, as a teacher, did not get angry with a student who played a wrong note or was unsuccessful in technique. However, he was displeased when a student would not put his emotion and expression into the music. This is an interesting parallel to many good teachers' classroom mannerisms. They do not scold a child who makes a mistake at a new concept, but do get discouraged when a student doesn't try at what he/she does.

Self-confidence was something Beethoven did not lack when it came to his music. He knew he had a gift and he would not let anyone or anything get in the way of composing his music. Beethoven was the leader of a new kind of composer. Until his time, composers were like servants: paid to write and perform music for the rich. Beethoven challenged that idea by writing music for himself first and an audience second. Some people at this time didn't understand or appreciate the music they heard at concerts and recitals. In fact, audience members had been known to walk out of recitals disappointed at what they had paid to hear. This frustrated Beethoven not because these people didn't accept his music, but because they didn't understand it and they were losing out.

Beethoven did act somewhat as he is personified by the popular media of today. He was known to break pianos and piano strings by playing the keys with intensity. In fact, it was because of Beethoven that the need for a stronger structure of the piano arose. Many contemporaries thought him to be rash and ill-mannered. Beethoven was embarrassed to be with people because of his hearing loss. But those who knew his music heard the man within. Beethoven used his music to express himself. His music acts as an autobiography of emotions: dilemmas, joys, disappointments and finally inner peace. Beethoven's life seemed to be a series of obstacles to overcome, but he did overcome them with music as his constant companion.

Beethoven's death can be considered as stormy as much of his life. While lying on his death bed, surrounded by his nephew, Karl and dearest friends, a thunderstorm broke out. Karl later wrote in a journal that his uncle sat up as lightning struck, shook his fist, fell back in his bed and died. Though the man was now gone, his music still remains some of the most well-known. Among them are *Für Elise,* the first movement of his piano sonata, *Moonlight Sonata,* the first movement of his *Fifth Symphony*, and his *Ninth Symphony* which embodies the ever recognizable melody, *Ode to Joy.*

As a child, Frederic Chopin (1810-1849) showed a profound love for music. His first teacher was his older sister, Ludwika, who taught him for less than a year before Chopin outgrew her instruction. He then went on to private lessons with an expert Warsaw musician. Chopin began being pointed out to local nobility as a piano prodigy and expert in the works of the masters.

At twenty, Chopin left his Polish homeland to live in Paris which at the time was the center of artistic expression. However, Chopin's love and devotion for Poland never ceased. Before he left his homeland, the people of Poland presented him with a precious gift of a silver urn filled with Polish dirt so that he would always have a piece of his beloved Poland with him. This prized possession was kept faithfully in Chopin's home and when Chopin died, the urn was buried with him in Paris. Much of his music expresses these feelings of nationalism towards Poland.

Chopin's fame in Paris spread slowly as he earned his living by teaching. The salons of the great and major concert halls of Europe were soon opened to him; however, Chopin preferred the intimacy of playing for smaller audiences best.

Chopin composed slowly, as he was a perfectionist. His music was tender and filled with emotional qualities. Often his performances would bring tears to his listeners' eyes. Among his admirers were fellow romantic composers Franz Liszt and Felix Mendelssohn; poet Victor Hugo; and woman novelist George Sand who had taken a man's name in order for her work to sell. Chopin and George fell in love.

Chopin was a sickly man and after a concert tour of England in 1848, he fell seriously ill. George spent much time trying to nurse him back to health, but soon he was diagnosed with tuberculosis. Chopin died in 1849 at the young age of thirty-nine.

From the age of eight, Chopin's goal in life was to compose, his works written exclusively for his beloved instrument, the solo piano. He is nicknamed "The Poet of the Piano." His repertoire of piano compositions includes numerous polonaises, waltzes, etudes, nocturnes and preludes. His music's sensitive, lyrical, and melancholy qualities show through in every piece and establish him firmly as the ideal representation of music in the Romantic age.

At the age of seven, Russian-born Peter Ilyich Tchaikovsky (1840-1893) begged for piano lessons after hearing Mozart's *Don Giovanni* on a music box. Though he did begin piano lessons, his father was not happy with young Peter's excitement with music and did not encourage him. Instead, he pushed Peter to go to law school. Begrudgingly, he did. However, after his mother's death, the pull towards composition was too great and he began writing his first pieces as he decided to make music a major part in his life.

In 1862, Tchaikovsky entered the St. Petersburg Conservatory as a music student studying under Anton Rubenstein. While in school, Tchaikovsky earned money by giving music lessons and once he graduated, he began teaching harmony at the Moscow Conservatory.

Tchaikovsky was a very shy man who expressed many of his emotions through music. He married once in 1877, but the marriage lasted only three short weeks. This and other personal periods of turmoil left Tchaikovsky nearing a mental breakdown. It was music that helped him in times of despair.

In 1876, Tchaikovsky began a lifelong friendship with the wealthy Nadezhda von Meck. Their relationship was very odd. They communicated through letter writing alone and often Mrs. von Meck would offer Tchaikovsky the chance to stay at one of her properties, but only when she was not there. They never met, however, Mrs. von Meck commissioned Tchaikovsky to transcribe much of his work into piano arrangements for her. Eventually, she volunteered to pay Tchaikovsky yearly so that he could give up teaching and devote all his time to composing. Under Mrs. von Meck's financial backing, Tchaikovsky was able to compose many magnificent works.

Among some of Tchaikovsky's most famous works are *Swan Lake, Sleeping Beauty* and *The Nutcracker* ballets, *The 1812 Overture,* and six symphonies including his sixth and final, the *Pathétique.* He was most proud of this last symphony. It is a tribute to his life. Among the places he traveled, including Germany, Austria-Hungary, France and England, he visited America in 1891 to conduct a dedication concert at the Carnegie Hall in New York.

John Phillip Sousa (1854-1932), born

in Washington, D.C., was originally trained as a violinist and also enjoyed playing the piano and some wind instruments. By the age of thirteen, he became a member of the United States Marine Band, the official band of the President of the United States. By 26, he was the leader. When he first became leader, he had an ordinary band, but he shaped them into the finest in the country. He drilled them until he heard perfection and expanded their repertoire by ordering new music and composing some of his own, including: *The Washington Post March, The Semper Fidelis March* and *Stars and Stripes Forever*. He is now known as "The March King," and his music is heard every July 4th and at numerous military and patriotic events.

There are few things known about Claude Debussy (1862-1918) since most was mysteriously concealed. However, some things have been discovered about his musical life and his emergence as a musician. He was brought up with his formal education neglected, beginning piano lessons at nine years of age in Cannes, France. In 1873, he entered the Paris Conservatoire and spent eleven years studying piano and theory. He was a good pianist, but reports indicate that he was "eccentric." "He astounded us all by his bizarre playing," said a fellow pupil, "he literally charred the piano. He seemed enraged with the instrument, treating it roughly and impulsively, and breathing loudly as he played different passages." He became know as the "*enfant terrible,*" exclaiming things such as, "Why must dissonant chords always be resolved?" He was a serious student most of the time. The rest of the time he acted as the class clown performing mock lessons when teachers' backs were turned.

As a child, Debussy collected butterflies, loving their colors. He wanted to be a painter. Being influenced by French impressionistic painters Cezanne and Monet, Debussy began composing music that painted pictures. This impressionistic style of composition was received by audiences with varying responses: some enjoyed it, many hated and ridiculed it. Not many people accepted Debussy as a serious composer and, unfortunately, his talent wasn't appreciated until after he died. However, Debussy has become the leading figure in music in the style of "Impressionism" by his ability to arouse the imagination with his music. Some of his most well-known impressionistic pieces are: *Prelude to the Afternoon of a Faun, The Girl with the Flaxen Hair, Clouds* and the quite famous *Clair de Lune,* that can be heard in various commercials and movies.

Scott Joplin (1868–1917) was born in Texas, the son of former slaves, when the roots of the ragtime style of music was still being formed. His father, a fiddler by hobby, didn't believe that a black man could make a respectable living from music. His mother, a banjo player by hobby, saw it differently and enjoyed cleaning the house to Scott's piano playing. She worked hard to keep Scott in piano lessons, but soon teachers wanted to teach him for free!

At seventeen Scott left home to tour the Midwest with his Texas Medley Quartet. During their travels they heard many new sounds emerging. The most exciting of these was a jerky sound known as "jug piano" played by a growing number of black musicians. The sound featured a non-stop syncopation that accented the beats in a measure that were normally weak. This syncopation became known as "ragged time" and eventually "ragtime." Although to some Joplin was the "King of Ragtime" and "The Entertainer," few recognized his genius. His music was considered inferior to classical music by the elite and too serious to be popular dance tunes. Besides the *Maple Leaf Rag*, none of his other 50 published rags were big hits and only three were recorded during his lifetime. Now, Joplin is extremely well-known and loved and the genre of Ragtime is virtually synonymous with the name of Scott Joplin.

When George Gershwin (1898–1937) was a young boy, he believed that music was for girls and wanted no part in it. Instead, he was busy playing stickball, baseball and keeping his title of roller-skating champion in his neighborhood. But when he was ten, he heard one of his classmates play Dvorak's *Humoresque* and was drawn into the beauty of music. George's older brother, Ira, had already been interested in music and was taking piano lessons. Soon, George convinced his parents to let him take lessons too. He worked for hours on the piano writing songs and working in music stores. By the time he was nineteen, George had become rich and famous from his first hit, *Swanee*. The two brothers became great partners. Ira was known as "Mr. Words" and George was known as "Mr. Music." Together, they wrote many Broadway musicals including *Girl Crazy, Funny Face, Of Thee I Sing* and the opera, *Porgy and Bess*.

Duke Ellington (1899–1974) was a young boy who hated his piano lessons. He didn't seem to understand why he needed to be taught in such a structured manner and lost interest quickly. Ironically, once he stopped taking lessons, he really began to make music. He enjoyed playing at the keyboard and improvising at the piano. His talent was evident and it took him places. He started by playing at parties, pool halls, and clubs and soon formed his own band in Washington, D.C. Soon, his band traveled to Harlem, New York, where they played jazz music in various clubs. One club, The Cotton Club, was a regular gig and soon their nightly performances were broadcast live on the radio. This made Ellington's music very well-known. He continued to compose and collaborate with other musicians. Among his great repertoire of compositions are *Take the "A" Train, It Don't Mean a Thing (If It Ain't Got That Swing), I'm Beginning to See the Light,* and *Prelude to a Kiss*.

Aram Khachaturian, (1903–1978) an Armenian composer, showed an early love of music but no particular talent or ambition. He played the tenor horn in the school band and taught himself a little piano. At age nineteen, Khachaturian went to Moscow ignorant of music and was admitted to Gnessin's Music School, where he studied cello for three years, as well as composition with Gnessin himself. In 1929, he transferred to the Moscow Conservatory and studied composition and orchestration. Among his works are incidental music written for productions of the Moscow Art Theatre, the Vakhtangov Theatre and the Armenian State Theatre. He wrote scores for several films as well, including *Pepo,* from which one theme song became one of Armenia's national songs. He also wrote *Sabre Dance* and the music of the movie *Spartacus*. Khachaturian's music is deeply rooted in and influenced by the traditions of his native Armenia as well as that of Russia, Azerbaijan, the Ukraine and Turkey. Born in the Georgian capital of Tiflis, now Tbilisi, he grew up in "an atmosphere rich in folk music, festivities, rituals, joyful and tragic events in the life of the people … impressions that became engraved on my memory and determined my musical thinking … the natural soil nourishing my work." Among several of his Soviet awards, he received the "People's Artist" award.

Ella Fitzgerald (1918-1996) came into the life of music by a true twist of fate. At the age of 16,

Ella had entered into a talent show at the Apollo Theater in Harlem as a dancer. Once on stage, she froze. From backstage, the Master of Ceremonies urged her to do something and so a frightened little Ella opened up her mouth, let go, and sang. Immediately she was loved by the audience. Benny Carter, a composer, sax player, musical arranger and member of the Apollo audience that day, especially took an interest in her talent. He introduced her to many of the big names in Harlem's music scene. Ella won that talent show and went on to win many more.

Ella is well-known for her talents in improvisation and scat singing (singing nonsense words in a way that imitates an instrument). She could improvise a melody brilliantly while on stage, in the true style of a great jazz musician. Her scat singing can be considered an art form all its own. Through a lifetime of performances that spanned six decades and worldwide praise from fans, Ella remained humble, never calling herself a musician. However, she will forever be revered as "The First Lady of Jazz," as she is respected and admired by some of the greatest American musicians and music critics.

Peggy Lee (1920-2002) withstood a hard life as a child. When little Norma was four, her

mother died and after her father remarried, she had to suffer under the hand of an abusive stepmother.

Through it all, she found peace in music, especially singing. In her teens, Norma continued to develop her voice and style while she listened to Count Basie's orchestra on the radio. Finally, she had the opportunity to sing her debut on a local radio station, KOVC. Later at an audition with WDAY in Fargo, ND, Norma showed so much personality, style and desire that the station's program director of WDAY suggested that she use the name Peggy Lee. And that's how she was introduced on the air. From there, Peggy sang at local gigs and soon had an audition with a Chicago club. It was there that she was singing with Benny Goodman's orchestra. They recorded hits together and went on tour. Duke Ellington, after hearing a performance in New York declared, "If I'm the Duke, man, Peggy Lee is the queen."

Peggy was not only a vocalist, but also a poet, author, painter, greeting card designer and composer, composing many of the songs she recorded. When Walt Disney made the cartoon classic "Lady and the Tramp," they called on Peggy's talent. She wrote many of the original songs, including the *Siamese Cat Song* and was the voice of many of the characters.

Peggy Lee is one of the most well know jazz vocalists in American music history. Her feverish singing style gave her an amazing 50-year career that included jazz, blues, swing, Latin and rock. She recorded over 650 songs, more than 60 albums and remained an active musician until her death in 2003. Her unmistakable, voice, however lives on as she is one of jazz's legends.

Name: _____ Class: _____ Date: _____

Key Words: (Composers)/Music/Genres

Name the ___composer___ .

  1. prodigy, laugh, orchestra   _____

  2. wig, church, violin   _____

  3. piano, symphony, bold   _____

  4. no wig, Germany, deaf   _____

  5. piano, Poland, no wig   _____

  6. 20 kids, church, organ   _____

  7. Venice, priest, red hair   _____

  8. waltz, "poet", 39   _____

Now you make one:

___composer___ :   _____

key words: _____, _____,

_____

Use this to quiz your students on composers. These key words will test their understanding of the differences among composers. This is an example. Use the next page to make one of your own using key words that you and your class make up. You may also use the next page the same way only for different pieces of music or genres of music.

Answers: 1. Mozart, 2. Vivaldi, 3. Beethoven, 4. Beethoven, 5. Chopin, 6. Bach, 7. Vivaldi, 8. Chopin

Inspired by Listening

Key Words: Composers/Music/Genres

Name the _____ .

1. _____,_____,_____   _____

2. _____,_____,_____   _____

3. _____,_____,_____   _____

4. _____,_____,_____   _____

5. _____,_____,_____   _____

6. _____,_____,_____   _____

7. _____,_____,_____   _____

8. _____,_____,_____   _____

Now you make one:

_____ : _____

key words: _____ _____

_____

Composer Project

~Overview~

Use this "composer project" to help your students learn about different composers and their music. Here is a brief overview of the following pages:

- Contents of Packet sheet (page 137) – Use this to inform students about what materials are provided for them in their packets.
- The following are materials that you will need to make available to your students for the project. They will be collected at the conclusion of the project.
    - Picture of Composer
    - Informational Articles about Composer – If you are limited by time or availability of research materials, you may want to provide the information for the students to look through.

        If you would rather, have students do the research at the library or in the computer lab. If you do this, you may want to have the appropriate resources ready for them. For example, have a cart or display of appropriate books at their disposal or make a folder of websites in the favorites list on their computers so that they have only to click on a link to get the information they need. This helps cut down on time that could be better spent researching instead of searching.
    - Recording of Composer's Music – A copy of a recording you own will do. Recordings that are a sampling of the composer's music are best. You may also want to provide students with the option of finding music on the internet. Again, having website addresses ready for them is best.
    - Instruction Sheet (page 138)
- Job Sheet (139) – This paper helps students get organized and understand what is involved with the project.
- Biography Sheet (140) – This paper helps students gather their ideas about the composer.
- Piece Sheet (141) – This paper helps students gather their ideas about the piece.
- Note Cards for Presentation – In my experience, it is best to give these to students only when they are ready to finalize what they will say.

Ideas for the Teacher:

- Group the students first. There should be 4 to a group. One or two groups may have 5.
- Take the time to go over the project in detail and to answer questions.
- Use the job sheet as a sort of rubric to grade the students. Let the students know you will do this.
- Once the 4 classes are completed, use the next two classes to present the projects.
- Use the evaluation sheet (page 142) as a quiz for the students to take after they have all presented their projects. This will help you know if they all really did participate. All students should be sharing information with one another. You can let students know this is coming.

Composer Project

Contents of Packet

Picture of Composer
Informational Articles about Composer
Recording of Composer's Music
Instruction Sheet
Job Sheet
Biography Sheet
Piece Sheet

Your Composer is

_____

Instructions

Your group will begin a project on a composer today. Your project will consist of three parts.
1. Biographical Information about Your Composer
2. Visual Presentation
3. Piece of Music by Your Composer

Each person in your group will have a job since you will only have 4 class periods to prepare your presentation. The **JOB SHEET** will help you organize this part. Sometimes it will be necessary for a person to take on two or more jobs. Other times it will be necessary for a job to be completed by more than one person. Pick your leader first and then pick people for the other jobs.

This is a detailed outline of the three parts of your project.
1. Biographical Information about Your Composer
   a. Use the informational articles in this packet to find information about your composer. The **BIOGRAPHY SHEET** will help you find out some key information.
   b. Put the information you will use for your presentation on the **NOTE CARDS** so that it will be easy to present the information you found.
2. Visual Presentation
   a. For this part of the project, you need to make a visual presentation. This could be a poster, a sculpture, a mobile, diorama, painting or any other interesting visual you can think of to present to the class. Be creative and original!
   b. During your presentation to the class, you will need to explain briefly what your visual is and how it relates to your composer.
3. Piece of Music by Your Composer
   a. When it is your day to listen, your entire group will have a chance to listen to some music by your composer. At this time you will listen to the various pieces on the recording and pick ONE for your focus.
   b. Use the **PIECE SHEET** to help you when you write about the piece. Put this information on **NOTE CARDS** to help you when you present the piece to the class.

Try to work out any questions and problems with your group BEFORE seeing me. I will be roaming around and will check in with you. If your group needs to discuss something with me, the leader should act as spokesperson.

Good luck and have fun!

Job Sheet

JOB TITLE	RESPONSIBILITIES	NAME
Leader	1. Complete this job sheet. 2. Make sure people are doing what they need to do. 3. Make sure your project is completed on time. 4. Set up time for listening. 5. Act as "alternate" if a person is absent. 6. Act as spokesperson for group. 7. Introduce the composer to the class during your final presentation. 8. Keep your presentation flowing. 9. Let the class know when your presentation is done.	
Biographical Researchers	1. Read through the informational articles. 2. Complete the BIOGRAPHY SHEET. 3. Do something interesting with the information for your presentation. 4. Present biographical information during your final presentation.	
Artists	1. Decide on the visual presentation and clear it with the leader. 2. Discuss the composer with the researchers to get information to use in the visual. 3. Design and make the visual. 4. Present your artwork as part of your final presentation.	
Listeners	1. Once the piece is determined, listeners listen to the piece many times. 2. Complete the PIECE SHEET. 3. Do something interesting with the information for your presentation. 4. Present information and music during your final presentation.	

Other things I will look for:
1. Self-motivation
2. Effort
3. Quality of Work
4. Work Ethic

Things you ALL should know:
1. Composer's name and how to spell it.
2. Name of the piece and how to spell it.
3. Basic and interesting facts about your composer.

Names: _____ Class: _____ Date: _____

Biography Sheet

1. Name of composer: _____

2. Place and date of birth: _____, _____

3. What was happening in the world when your composer was alive?_____
   _____
   _____

4. How did your composer start to be interested in music?
   _____
   _____

5. Anything interesting about your composer's family?
   _____
   _____

6. Who influenced your composer?_____
   _____

7. What are some highlights of your composer's musical career? (at least 3)
   - _____
     _____
   - _____
     _____
   - _____
     _____
   - _____
     _____

8. How and when did your composer die? _____
   _____

9. What is something else that you found that was interesting about your composer?
   _____
   _____

10. What makes your composer different from other composers? _____
    _____
    _____
    _____

Names: _____ Class: _____ Date: _____

Piece Sheet

1. What is the composer's name? _____

2. What is the name of the piece you picked? _____

3. Why did your group pick this piece of music? _____

4. Listen to the piece at least three times and write down a few images or words that come to mind when you hear it.

_____

5. For the next part, you will listen to the piece and start to make up a paragraph for the presentation. In your paragraph you will need to use at least 6 of the vocabulary words learned in class to describe the piece.

Word: _____ - _____
_____

Word: _____ - _____
_____

Word: _____ - _____
_____

Word: _____ - _____
_____

Word: _____ - _____
_____

Word: _____ - _____
_____

When you present your piece to the class follow these steps:
- Tell the class why your group picked this piece.
- Tell the class what kinds of images you think of when you listen to the piece.
- Read your paragraph slowly to the class.

Name: _____ Class: ____ Date: _____

Composer Project Evaluation Sheet

Name of your composer: _____

Give three facts about your composer:

1. _____
2. _____
3. _____

What was the name of the piece your group presented?

_____

Name the people in your group and what they did to help complete the project:

1. _____, _____
2. _____, _____
3. _____, _____
4. _____, _____
5. _____, _____

What did you do? _____

What part of your job did you like? Why? _____

_____

What part didn't you like? Why? _____

_____

What part of your job did you do well? _____

_____

If you were to do this project again what would you do differently? Why?

_____

_____

Musical Genres

These are short explanations of a few of the genres of music. When picking out music, don't limit yourself to these genres only. Bring in all kinds of music to keep your students' interest and motivation. Don't be afraid to try something new or share music you enjoy, even if you think your students may not. Your enthusiasm may be just what they need to open their ears to new kinds of music and inspire them to listen.

Baroque (1600-1750)
In this period of music, the major and minor scales came to replace the older church modes. Italian words and their musical meaning, such as *forte* and *piano* became important notations for performers. Such musical decoration as the "trill" became the fashion and the violin became the queen of instruments. At this time in history, composers were paid servants whose job was to write music for nobility, play at parties or compose for church services.

The Baroque period received its name from a term used to describe over-decorated church architecture. It is also Italian for the "pearl," which is noted for its "imperfect beauty." You can hear these decorative embellishments in much of the music from this period. It is the beginning of almost all musical styles up to the present.

Noteworthy Baroque composers: Bach, Vivaldi, Handel, Purcell

Classical (1750-1825)
In this period of music, contrast in dynamics, register and mood within a piece were popular musical devises. Composers favored the sonata form and the string quartet was a favorite ensemble for which to write music. The piano was invented, which replaced the harpsichord as a keyboard instrument of choice. The piano, unlike any other keyboard instrument before it, could play a range of dynamics (loud and soft) and a wider range of pitches (high and low).

The Classical period is noted for its changes in feelings and ideas as it embodies the historical events of the Industrial, French and American Revolutions. Artists and architects used less embellishing styles and writers swayed to a simpler, more concise manner of communicating thoughts. Musicians preferred music that was balanced and structured. Sounds of rebellion, patriotism, and individualism were a common theme among composers. At the beginning of this period composers were still hired as servants to the wealthy and the church. Yet, as the period progresses, composers began to write music for their own satisfaction and that of the general public.

The first public concerts where held in this time period as a means to entertain the masses, not just the aristocrats. The first musical publications were also made available to the general public during this time period.

Noteworthy Classical composers: Haydn, Mozart, Beethoven

Romantic (late 1700's–1900) In this period music became personal and subjective, as composers began to write for their own expression and not simply as a servant composing for individual, rich patrons.

The Romantic period rebels against the structured, disciplined music of the classical era and leans toward freedom of expression, describing music as the language of human emotion. The music becomes poetic as it mirrors the personality of the composer. Composers are free to express themselves through their music rather than write music only for special occasions.

Noteworthy Romantic composers: Beethoven (later compositions), Chopin, Liszt, Schumann, Berlioz, Brahms, Wagner, Verdi

Modern (early 1900's–) In this period of music, dissonance is allowed, major and minor scales are not always the foundation of a piece and traditional ideas about rhythm, melody and harmony are challenged.

The Modern period's composers explore new techniques of composition and instrumentation, trying to find new ways to express their ideas. For example, composers may instruct the performers to play a traditional instrument in a non-traditional manner such as playing a violin with the back side of the bow. Modern composers like to challenge the listener's ears by experimenting with new sounds.

Noteworthy Modern composers: Debussy, Ravel, Prokofiev, Satie, Bartok, Stravinsky, Schoenberg, Copland, Cage, Gershwin

A Symphony is a large work that is made up of 4 separate sections called movements. These movements each sound differently than the next but they all flow together as they are considered pieces of a whole, like chapters of a book. The first movement generally has a fast tempo and grabs the audience's attention. The second movement contrasts the first in that it is slow and lyrical. The third movement has a dance-like quality as it is written in ¾ time, the time signature of a waltz or minuet. The fourth movement is generally quick and loud; a grand finale, if you will, such as you would see in a fireworks display.

The Symphony is mostly considered a classical form of music as it underwent the most development in the Classical time period. Haydn wrote 104 symphonies, becoming the expert who perfected the form of the orchestral work. Beethoven had the greatest influence on the symphony in the 9 that he wrote. He stretched the musical form's boundaries, challenging the traditional ways of composing a symphony. In his last symphony, *Symphony #9*, Beethoven added soloists and a complete chorus, along with the orchestra.

Noteworthy symphonies: Mozart's *Symphony No.40 in g minor, K 550*; Haydn's *Farewell Symphony*; Beethoven's *5th Symphony* and *9th Symphony, Choral*.

Opera is a combination of stage action, scenic effects and music. The difference between opera and a staged musical is that in an opera **all** the words are sung, with only the occasional spoken dialogue (if at all).

The text of an opera is called the libretto. There are two types of sung libretto in an opera: aria and recitative. An aria is a melodic piece sung by one or more actors. A recitative is a sort of speech song which has no real form or melodic line. Both types are sung to orchestral accompaniment. Often an opera will be made up of many arias connected by small sections of recitative and choral embellishments.

Operas can be tragic or happy, comedic or deeply philosophical, simple or complex in accompaniment. There is no such thing as a typical opera.

Noteworthy Operas: Mozart's *The Magic Flute,* Verdi's *La Traviata*, Rossini's *The Barber of Seville,* Bizet's *Carmen,* Puccini's *Madame Butterfly*

Program Music is music that attempts to paint a picture, describe an action, or tell a story without using words. A composer may try to imitate the sound of birds chirping or to recreate a battle scene. Drumming suggests soldiers marching; a flute, the song of birds. Often a composer will give a descriptive name to his/her piece in order to help the listener get the full effects of the music.

Noteworthy compositions:
Beethoven, *Pastoral Symphony*
Berlioz, *Symphonie Fantastique*
Mendelssohn, *Songs Without Words*
Schubert, *Gretchen at the Spinning Wheel*
Saint-Saens, *Danse Macabre*
Debussy, *Clair de Lune*
Rimsky-Korsakov, *The Flight of the Bumblebee*
Bartok, *The Fly*

Teaching about Genres of Music

~Overview~

The following is an example unit that I used in my music classes to give my students a general overview of the four major genres (time periods) in music history. Of course, you may want to use this outline for other genres of music like jazz, rock or whatever else you may be studying. Here is a basic outline of how I taught this unit using Baroque, Classical, Romantic and Modern music.

Unit Outline

First Lesson

Objectives
STUDENTS WILL:
- Gain a general idea of the four major genres of music history we will study.
- Begin to understand how each genre was a reaction to those before it.
- Create visual representations of each genre.

Procedures:
1. Pass out the packet made of the cover sheet (149) and four copies of the genres paper found on pages 150-151.
2. Introduce the names of the four genres: Baroque, Classical, Romantic and Modern.
3. Give a quick, general overview of each genre. Students should write the name of the genre on the cover and the corresponding page, write down the general summary of the genre and then start to work on the cover illustration for that genre.

   For example, Baroque:
   - Explain that in the Baroque genre, music was often ornamented.
   - Have students write that down next to the first bullet on their Baroque page of the packet and then write the word Baroque in the "Baroque style" on the cover. (Students may write the letters of the word in swirly print. See the student examples on page 152 to get a more detailed idea.)
4. Continue going over the genres, stopping after each general explanation for students to write down notes and start illustrations. At the end, allow students time to finish their cover illustrations.

Informative Lessons

Objectives
STUDENTS WILL:
- Learn more details about the music of the genre.
- Learn about 2 composers or musicians of the genre.
- Actively listen to key examples of music from the genre.
- Summarize information about the genre, its composers and music.

Materials:

- Packets
- Highlighters/Markers
- Index cards cut in half for flash cards
- Envelopes for students to keep their flash cards
- Recording of exemplary music

Procedures:

1. Take 2 classes (or more, depending on your needs) for each genre to go over the important information about it by focusing on one composer or musician and his/her music each class.
2. During the 3rd class, summarize that genre by doing the following:
   - Decide on a color that represents the genre. Use this color to do the highlighting of key words and the creating of the flash cards.
   - Highlight key words in the main characteristics section.
   - Make flash cards for composers (use key words and phrases from the notes).
   - Summarize by finishing the sentences on the composer side of the pages.
3. At the beginning of the next class, before you start the next genre, students will take a 5-minute quiz on the genre from the previous class. Examples of these quizzes are on pages 153-154. You may use these or you may want to make your own, depending on what you focus on during your lessons.

Sum-Up Lesson

Objectives
STUDENTS WILL:

- Construct a table with summarizing information about the genres, composers and music.
- Further understand the progression of and relationship among the genres.

Materials:

- Markers
- Packets
- Student made flash cards
- Sum-Up papers (pages 155-159)

Procedures:

1. Break the class up into 4 groups. Each group is assigned one genre.
2. Give each group the paper for the genre they are assigned.
3. Students work together to complete the paper for their genre.
4. When students are done with their genre, they write their answers on half sheets of 8½" x 11" paper. These papers should be attached to a larger table that has been created on a bulletin board.
5. If groups have extra time, they can work on filling out the rest of the table at their desks.
6. Once the big class table is complete, go over this with the class, reinforcing the progression of/relationship among the genres.
7. Spend any other time left in class to review anything else before the test.

Final Test

Take the test! An example test can be found on the pages 160 and 161.

This unit involves careful planning. You are teaching a lot of information in a short amount of time. Here is an idea of how you can tackle such a task.

Genre/ First Lesson Generalization	Other Characteristics of the Time	Composers and Their Music used in the Informative Lessons
Baroque Ornamentation, fancy, decorating music	Music for the aristocrats; terraced dynamics; no piano – harpsichord	Bach – *Toccata and Fugue in d minor, Little Fugue in g minor* Vivaldi – *Spring* from the *Four Seasons*
Classical Structured, followed a format	Music for the general public; first public concerts; first published music; piano invented	Haydn – Excerpts from the *Farewell Symphony* (great time to read <u>The Farewell Symphony</u> by Anna Harwell Celenza) Mozart – Excerpts from: *Symphony No. 40*, and *The Magic Flute* Beethoven – *Für Elise, 5th Symphony* (1st movement)
Romantic Expressing emotions	Rebellion against formalized art; piano most popular instrument; nationalism	Chopin – 1 waltz and 1 etude Liszt – *Hungarian Rhapsody*
Modern Breaking the rules, experimentation	Synthesizer, radio, record player are invented; music of the past is too predictable	Cage – *4'33"* (You may choose to perform this for the class yourself!) Debussy – *Clair de Lune*

How this fits with active listening

Here are a few ways to use this unit or parts of it if you are a music teacher or a general classroom teacher.

- As a follow up to this unit, you can do some active listening activities and lessons that use the music from the times, composers and genres you just studied.
- Use this unit after learning about active listening so that when your students get to listen to pieces of music they can listen actively.
- Extend this unit by inserting various active listening activities and lessons as you go through the various genres.
- Use this unit as a means to teach the background of the music in music class, allowing the classroom teacher to use that knowledge and active listening experiences to do various interpretation lessons.

Musical Genres

Name: _____ Class: _____

Date: _____

Genre:_____

Dates: _____

Genre:_____

Dates: _____

Genre :_____

Dates: _____

Genre:_____

Dates: _____

Main Characteristics:

- _____
  _____
- _____
  _____
- _____
  _____
- _____
  _____
- _____
  _____
- _____
  _____

Genre: _____

Composers/musicians of the _____ genre _____

_____

Major Composers/Musicians

The music of this genre _____

_____

_____

The Four Time Periods

Name: _____
Date: _____ Sec: _____

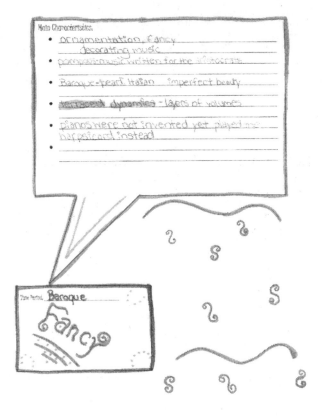

Composers of the _Romantic_ time period _1825-1900_

Major Composers

Chopin	• Piano • Poland (born) • Paris (died) • "Poet of the Piano"
1911-1886 France	• Born in Hungary, went to Vienna then Paris • Went through many pianos • Was called "The Piano Terminator" • Wrote unique and curious music • Toured Europe for 8 years

The Music of the times _____
_____
_____

Name: _____ Class: _____ Date: _____

Baroque Quiz

1. Two key facts about the Baroque genre:

- Write a key word that describes most Baroque music _____

- For what kind of people was most Baroque music written? _____

2. Which Baroque composer is which?

_____ red hair, Venice, worked at an orphanage

_____ wig, Germany, worked in various churches

_____ loved to play the violin

_____ the organ was his favorite

_____ he had 20 children

3. On the back doodle in the Baroque style…

Name: _____ Class: _____ Date: _____

Classical Quiz

1. Write two key facts about the Classical genre:

- Write a key word that describes most Classical music _____

- For what kind of people was most Classical music written? _____

2. Which Classical composer is which?

_____ was a child prodigy, traveled Europe at age 5

_____ composed 104 symphonies

_____ he became deaf, but continued to compose

_____ composed 9 symphonies

_____ was nicknamed the "Father of the Symphony"

> **Bonus:** What instrument was invented during this time period?
>
> _____

3. On the back doodle in the Classical style…

Name: _____ Class: _____ Date: _____

Romantic Quiz

1. Write two key facts about the Romantic genre:

- What did music written in the Romantic style allow composers to do? _____

- What word means that you show pride in your country?   N_____

2. Which Romantic composer is which?

_____ he ONLY composed for the piano

_____ his nickname is the "Piano Terminator"

_____ he went into seclusion and practiced the piano for 8-12 hours a day

_____ his nickname is the "Poet of the Piano"

_____ he composed symphonies as well as piano music

3. On the back doodle in the Romantic style…

Name: _____ Class: _____ Date: _____

Modern Quiz

1. Write two key facts about the Modern genre:
- Modern composers liked to e_____ with new sounds.

- Name something that was invented during the modern time (music related). _____

2. Which Modern composer is which?

_____ he experimented with prepared pianos

_____ he painted pictures with his music

_____ he was considered an impressionistic composer

_____ he loved the idea of NOISE

_____ he was French

3. On the back doodle in the Modern style…

Time Period	Composers' Names	Who Composers Worked For/ How they Made Money	Who Music was Written For	Music of this Time was Meant to…	One Word Sum-Up of the Times
Baroque					
Classical					
Romantic					
Modern					

Time Period	Composers' Names	Who Composers Worked For/ How they Made Money	Who Music was Written For	Music of this Time was Meant to….	One Word Sum-Up of the Times
Baroque					
Classical					
Romantic					
MODern					

Name(s): _____   Class: _____ Date: _____

Time Period	Composers' Names	Who Composers Worked For/ How they Made Money	Who Music was Written For	Music of this Time was Meant to…	One Word Sum-Up of the Times
Baroque					
Classical					
Romantic					
MODern					

Name(s): _____

Class: _____ Date: _____

Time Period	Composers' Names	Who Composers Worked For/ How they Made Money	Who Music was Written For	Music of this Time was Meant to…	One Word Sum-Up of the Times
Baroque					
Classical					
Romantic					
MODern					

Name(s): _____

Class: _____ Date: _____

Time Period	Composers' Names	Who Composers Worked For/ How they Made Money	Who Music was Written For	Music of this Time was Meant to…	One Word Sum-Up of the Times
Baroque					
Classical					
Romantic					
MODern					

Name: _____ Class: _____ Date: _____

Test on the Four Major Genres of Music History and the Major Composers of those Genres

Match the composer with the genre:

1. Baroque _____ _____

2. Classical _____ _____

   _____

3. Romantic _____ _____

4. Modern _____ _____

> Composer Bank:
>
> Cage   Bach   Beethoven
>
> Haydn   Liszt   Chopin
>
> Mozart   Vivaldi   Debussy

Match the composer with his "instrument of choice."

5. Chopin _____

6. Bach _____

7. Vivaldi _____

> Instrument Bank:
>
> Organ   Violin   Piano

Match a composer with each fact. You may use an answer more than once. (Use the Composer bank above.)

8. _____ He is called the "Father of the Symphony."

9. _____ He was a priest who had red hair. His nickname was, *"Il Prete Rosso."*

10. _____ As a child, he copied music by the moonlight and, in doing so, memorized it.

11. _____ He worked in an orphanage for girls in Venice, Italy.

12. _____ He experimented with prepared pianos, unusual percussion instruments, electronics, weird notation and even silence.

13. _____ He is called the "Poet of the Piano."

14. _____ He is called the "Piano Terminator."

Match a composer with each fact. (cont.) You may use an answer more than once. (Use the Composer bank below.)

15. _____He did with music what impressionistic painters did with paint. He painted pictures with his music.

16. _____He went into seclusion and practiced the piano 8-12 hours a day because he wanted to be a piano virtuoso.

17. _____He was a child prodigy and toured Europe at the age of 5.

Composer Bank:
Cage   Bach   Beethoven
Haydn   Liszt   Chopin
Mozart   Vivaldi   Debussy

Match a genre with each fact. You may use an answer more than once. (Use the genre bank below.)

18. _____ The people thought that expressing their emotions was the most important thing.

Genres:
Baroque, Classical
Romantic, Modern

19. _____The people thought that structure and form was the most important thing.

20. _____The people thought that ornamentation was important in all art.

21. _____The people thought that it was time to experiment with different sounds in music.

22. _____The piano was invented during this genre's time period.

23. _____Music of this period sounded pompous, as it was written mostly for the aristocrats.

24. _____Music of this period was written for ordinary people; the middle class.

25. _____Nationalism, or love for one's country, was important during this genre's time period.

26. _____The harpsichord was used during this genre's time period. The piano had not been invented yet.

27. _____This genre was a direct rebellion against formalized art.

28. _____The first public concerts were given during this genre's time period.

Baroque Quiz

1. ornamentation (or other correct response); aristocrats
2. Vivaldi, Bach, Vivaldi, Bach, Bach

Classical Quiz

1. structured (or other correct response); general public
2. Mozart, Haydn, Beethoven, Beethoven, Haydn

Romantic Quiz

1. express emotions (or other correct response); Nationalism
2. Chopin, Liszt, Liszt, Chopin, Liszt

Modern Quiz

1. Experiment; there are many correct responses
2. Cage, Debussy, Debussy, Cage, Debussy

Final Test

1. Bach, Vivaldi
2. Haydn, Mozart, Beethoven
3. Chopin, Liszt
4. Cage, Debussy
5. piano
6. organ
7. violin
8. Haydn
9. Vivaldi
10. Bach
11. Vivaldi
12. Cage
13. Chopin
14. Liszt
15. Debussy
16. Liszt
17. Mozart
18. Romantic
19. Classical
20. Baroque
21. Modern
22. Classical
23. Baroque
24. Classical
25. Romantic
26. Baroque
27. Romantic (or Modern)
28. Classical

The Main Ingredients of Music

Rhythm

The steady **beat** of a piece of music is what drives the melody through time. Like our own heartbeat consistently beats from birth to death, the beat in music is constant throughout the piece from beginning to end. Also, like our heartbeat, musical beat can be fast, slow, or moderate and can speed up or slow down within a piece. The **tempo** is what controls the speed of music. "*Tempo*" in Italian means time. Often at the beginning of a piece of written music, there is a tempo marking. The tempo marking 60 is about the speed of a human heartbeat. When combining different note values, you can create different **rhythms** that lay over the steady heartbeat of music.

Melody

Melodies seem to float above all the other elements of music. Melody, usually found in the higher pitches of a piece of music, is the element that people tend to recognize first and is what most people can recall most easily. Think of the simple melodies you learned during your childhood: *Mary Had a Little Lamb, Row, Row, Row Your Boat; and Three Blind Mice*. All these are mostly memorable because of their melodies.

Melodies have shape. If you look at a melody on a written score of music and connect the note heads (like connect the dots) you can see how a melody moves up and down on the staff. This is the melody's **contour**. Sometimes the contour will move smoothly up and down like rolling hills, such as in Beethoven's *Ode to Joy*. Other times the contour can be jagged like a city skyline going from low to high notes and back again. Composers can also combine these contours to make new and interesting melodies.

Harmony

Harmony can give a sense of foundation to music or it can add a feeling of emotion. Anytime you have two or more pitches sounding at the same time, you have harmony. Notes are considered to be in **intervals** when they are sounded together. These intervals, or the distance between two notes, are named according to how many lines and spaces the notes are apart from each other on the staff. Two notes that are 6 lines and spaces away from each other (including the line or space the notes are on) are called a 6th. Two notes that are 3 lines and spaces away from each other are called a 3rd. Chords are also a main foundation of harmony. **Chords** are made up by playing three or more notes at the same time. Chords can be played in block fashion (notes played all at once) or can be broken up (notes of chord are played one after the other.)

In a lot of vocal music, both classical and popular, you may hear two or more voices harmonizing with each other. These voices are singing in varying intervals and the product is a beautiful sound. This type of harmonization can also be heard in instrumental music.

Dynamics

Dynamics are the louds and softs of music. Musicians use Italian words to describe dynamics in music. "*Forte*" means loud, "*piano*" means soft and if you put the word "*mezzo*" in front of either of those words, they mean medium loud or soft. You can also play something doubly soft or loud.

Symbol	*pp*	*p*	*mp*	*mf*	*f*	*ff*
Italian	Pianissimo	Piano	Mezzo Piano	Mezzo Forte	Forte	Fortissimo
English	Very Soft	Soft	Medium Soft	Medium Loud	Loud	Very Loud

There is also *crescendo* and *decrescendo* (or *diminuendo*). Crescendo means to gradually get louder. Decrescendo or diminuendo means to gradually get softer.

Crescendo: Decrescendo:

Tone Color (Timbre)

Tone color, also called **timbre** is the difference in sounds of instruments. A violin sounds different from a saxophone because they disperse different sound frequencies which in turn produce a different tone color. Many students can readily hear the differences among instruments. Tone color also refers to the differences in peoples' voices. Joe's voice will sound different from Brad's and they will both sound different from Milena.

Style

Style in music refers to everything from the differing styles of the composers to the styles of the times (how history shapes music).

Comparing dress style to musical style can be relevant. You probably dress differently from your students and maybe you enjoy different styles of music than they as well. Reinforce the idea that everyone needs to keep an open mind when it comes to musical style.

Lyrics

Lyrics are the words in music. Often you can read the lyrics of a song as if they were poetry. Poetry and lyrics can be similar in rhythm and rhyme. Many popular songs and raps are made of couplets, two lines of poetry where the end words rhyme with each other.

In the Classical and Romantic time periods, Art Songs were composed using popular poems of the day as the lyrics. In opera, the lyrics are called the "libretto."

Name: _____ Class: _____ Date: _____

The Main Ingredients of Music

Inspired by: _____ *by:* _____

Use this paper to define the elements of music as you hear them in the music. Describe what you hear in the piece of music.

Rhythm: _____

_____

Melody: _____

_____

Harmony: _____

_____

Dynamics: _____

_____

Tone Color: _____

_____

Style: _____

_____

Lyrics: _____ ____

_____

Draw a picture of what you imagine as you listen to the music.

Listening Suggestions

The following list of musical selections are only suggestions. My hope is that in looking for one of these pieces you will fall into a treasure trove of music you and your students will really enjoy. Many of the pieces are longer than what you would want to play for your class when you begin to share listening experiences with them. Don't let this discourage you from listening to those pieces, instead listen to an excerpt with your class. For example, Gershwin's *Rhapsody in Blue* is over 16 minutes long, however my students appreciate getting a taste of it since it is such a fun piece of music.

Bach, Johann Sebastian: *The Brandenburg Concertos, Jesu, Joy of Man's Desiring, Overture No. 3 in D major, Prelude in C major, Toccata and Fugue in D minor*

Beethoven, Ludwig van: *Für Elise, Minuet in G, "Moonlight" Sonata: Adagio sostenuto, Symphony No. 5: Allegro con brio,* excerpts from *Symphony No. 6 "Pastoral"*

Bizet, Georges: From the opera *Carmen: Children's March, Toreador Song, Habañera*

Chopin, Frederic: *Etude, Op. 10 No. 12 in c minor, Prelude No. 15 in D flat Major "Raindrops", Prelude No. 16 in b flat minor, Waltz No. 1 Op. 18 in E flat Major, Waltz No. 1, Op. 64 No. 1 in D flat Major*

Debussy, Claude: *Clair de Lune, The Girl with the Flaxen Hair, Minstrels, Prelude to The Afternoon of a Faun*

Ellington, Duke: *I'm Beginning to See the Light, It Don't Mean a Thing (If It Ain't Got That Swing), Prelude to a Kiss, Take the "A" Train*

Gershwin, George: *I Got Rhythm, The Man I Love, Rhapsody in Blue, Swanee, Someone to Watch Over Me*

Haydn, Franz Joseph: *Farewell Symphony, Surprise Symphony (2ⁿᵈ Movement)*

Holst, Gustav: *The Planets Suite*

Joplin, Scott: *The Entertainer, The Maple Leaf Rag, The Ragtime Dance, Weeping Willow*

Khachaturian, Aram: *Adventures of Ivan, Sabre Dance*

Liszt, Franz: *Hungarian Rhapsody No. 2*

Mendelssohn, Felix: Any of his *Songs Without Words: Confidence , Spinning Song, Venetian Gondola Songs, The Wedding March* from *Midsummer Night's Dream*

Miller, Glen: *Chattanooga Choo-Choo, In the Mood, (I've Got a Gal in) Kalamazoo, Moonlight Serenade, Pennsylvania 6-5000, Tuxedo Junction*

Mozart, Leopold: *"Toy" Symphony*

Mozart, Wolfgang Amadeus: *Eine Kleine Nachtmusik, Symphony No. 40 in g minor: Molto allegro, Turkish March, "Papageno's Song"* (from the opera *The Magic Flute), "Dies Irae"* and *"Lacrimosa"* (from *Mozart's Requiem*)

Rossini, Gioacchino: *William Tell Overture*

Schubert, Franz: *Ave Maria, Moment Musical No. 3 in f minor, Ständchen*

Strauss, Johann: *Annen Polka, The Blue Danube, Pizzicato Polka, Perpetuum Mobile Op. 257*

Stravinsky, Igor: *Firebird Suite, "Sacrificial Dance"* (from *The Rite of Spring)*

Tchaikovsky, Peter: *1812 Overture: Finale, Piano Concerto No. 1: Allegro non troppo,* sections from *The Sleeping Beauty* and *Swan Lake*

Vivaldi, Antonio: *Siciliano, The Four Seasons: Spring, Summer, Autumn, and Winter*

Wagner, Richard: *"Dance of the Prentices"* (from *Die Meistersinger von Nürnberg), "Ride of the Valkyries"* (from *Die Wülkure)*

CDs: When looking for a good CD of music to share with your class (or to enjoy on your own), look for the "Greatest Hits" types of CDs. The Greatest Hits of a composer or genre of music are great because they give you a taste of the more famous, popular and pleasing music. Look also for compilation, and collection CDs as well as CDs for children.

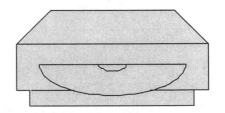

Picture Books: Biographical and for Enjoyment

Ackerman, Karen. <u>The Song and Dance Man</u>. New York: Alfred A. Knopf, 1988.

Anderson, M.T. <u>Handel, Who Knew What He Liked</u>. Cambridge, MA: Candlewick Press, 2001.

Anderson, M.T. <u>Strange Mr. Satie</u>. New York: Penguin Group, 2003.

Base, Graeme. <u>The Worst Band in the Universe</u>. New York: Harry N. Abrams, Inc., 1999.

Celenza, Anna Harwell. <u>Bach's Goldberg Variations</u>. Watertown, Massachusetts: Charlesbridge Imprint, 2005.

Celenza, Anna Harwell. <u>Gershwin's Rhapsody in Blue</u>. Watertown, Massachusetts: Charlesbridge Imprint, 2006.

Celenza, Anna Harwell. <u>The Heroic Symphony</u>. Watertown, Massachusetts: Charlesbridge Imprint, 2004.

Celenza, Anna Harwell. <u>The Farewell Symphony</u>. Watertown, Massachusetts: Charlesbridge Imprint, 2000.

Gatti, Anne. The Magic Flute. San Francisco, California: Chronicle Books, LLC: 1997.

Greene, Carol. Wolfgang Amadeus Mozart. Chicago: Children's Press, 1987.

Greene, Carol. John Philip Sousa, The March King. Chicago: Children's Press, 1992.

Isadora, Rachel. Young Mozart. New York: Penguin Books USA Inc., 1997.

Karlins, Mark. Music Over Manhattan. New York: Bantam Doubleday Dell Publishing Group, Inc., 1998.

Kroll, Steven. By the Dawn's Early Light. New York: Scholastic Inc., 1994.

Lepscky, Ibi. Amadeus Mozart. New York: Barron's Educational Series, Inc., 1982.

Lewiton, Mina. John Philip Sousa The March King. New York: Didier Publishing Co., 1944.

Lithgow, John. Carnival of the Animals. New York: Simon & Schuster Books for Young Readers, 2004.

McPhail, David. Mole Music. New York: Henry Holt and Co. Inc., 1999.

Moss, Lloyd. Zin! Zin! Zin! a Violin. New York: Simon & Schuster Books for Young Readers, 1995.

Orgill, Roxane. If I Only Had a Horn, Young Louis Armstrong. Boston: Houghton Mifflin Co., 1997.

Pinkney, Andrea Davis. Duke Ellington. New York: Hyperion Books for Children, 1998.

Pinkney, Andrea Davis. Ella Fitzgerald, The Tale of a Vocal Virtuosa. New York: Hyperion Books for Children, 2002.

Raschka, Chris. Charlie Parker Played Be Bop. New York: Orchard Books, 1992.

Spier, Peter (Illustrator). The Star-Spangled Banner. New York: Dell Publishing, 1973.

Weatherford, Carole Boston. The Sound that Jazz Makes. New York: Walker & Co., 2000.

Winter, Jeanette. Sebastian: A Book About Bach. New York: Browndeer Press, 1999.

Informational Books to get Students Acquainted with Music and Composers

Aliki. Ah, Music. New York: HarperCollins Publishers, 2003.

Bye, L. Dean. Student's Guide to the Great Composers. Montana: Mel Bay Publications, 1988.

Kinghorn, Harriet; Jacqueline Badman, and Lisa Lewis-Spicer. Let's Meet Famous Composers. Minnesota: T. S. Denison & Company, Inc., 1992.

Levine, Robert. The Story of the Orchestra. New York: Black Dog & Leventhal Publishers, Inc., 2001.

Osborne, Charles. The Dictionary of Composers. New York: Barnes & Noble Books, 1981.

Rachlin, Ann. <u>Famous Children</u>. New York: Barron's Educational Series. (Series includes: Bach, Beethoven, Chopin, Mozart, Schubert, Handel, Brahms, Schumann, Tchaikovsky, and Haydn.)

Venezia, Mike. <u>Getting to Know the World's Greatest Composers</u>. Chicago: Children's Press. (Series includes Beethoven and Mozart.)

<u>Black Americans of Achievement</u> series. New York: Chelsea House Publishers. (Includes books on: Louis Armstrong, Count Bassie, John Coltrane, Duke Ellington, Ella Fitzgerald, Dizzy Gillespie, Billie Holiday, Lena Horne, Scott Joplin.)

Reference Books for You

Ammons, Mark, <u>Music Activity Book</u>. Mark Twain Media, Inc., 1995.

Campbell, Don. <u>The Mozart Effect, Tapping the Power of Music to Heal the Body, Strengthen the Mind and Unlock the Creative Spirit</u>. New York: Avon Books, 1997.

Campbell, Don. <u>The Mozart Effect for Children: Awakening Your Child's Mind, Health, and Creativity with Music</u>. New York: HarperCollins Publishers Inc., 2000.

Campbell, Patricia Shehan and Carol Scott-Kasser. <u>Music in Childhood, From Preschool Through the Elementary Grades</u>. New York: Schirmer Books, 1995.

Copland, Aaron. <u>What to Listen for in Music</u>. New York: Penguin Putnam, Inc., 1939.

De Souza, Chris. <u>Exploring the Arts: Listening to Music</u>. New York: Marshall Cavendish Corp., 1989.

Gardner, Howard. <u>Multiple Intelligences, The Theory in Practice</u>. New York: BasicBooks, 1993.

Goldfluss, Karen (Editor). <u>Focus on Composers</u>. Westminster, California: Teacher Created Materials, Inc., 2000.

Kinghorn, Harriet; Jacqueline Badman, and Lisa Lewis-Spicer. <u>Let's Meet Famous Composers</u>. Minneapolis, Minnesota: T. S. Denison & Company, Inc., 1992.

Storr, Anthony. <u>Music and the Mind.</u> New York: Random House, 1992.

Where to find Fun Music Toys and Instruments

www.musiciselementary.com

www.friendshiphouse.com

www.themusicstand.com

Internet Websites with Information and Games

Note Practice
http://www.happynote.com/music/learn.html
Download free, fun games to practice your note reading skills including 'Notes in Space' and 'Note Tetris.'

Online Music Theory Reference
http://www.teoria.com/reference/index.htm
Look up information on music theory.

Complete music reference that is fun too!
http://www.town4kids.com/town4kids/kids/music4kids/musicfront.htm
Learn about everything from music theory to the great composers to instruments to music from different cultures.

Composer Information
http://www.classicalarchives.com
A collection of sound clips from famous pieces by the great composers.

http://www.composers.net
A collection of web pages that give a lot of information about composers including biographies, articles and sound clips.

http://archiv.radio.cz/hudba/indexeng.html
A quick and detailed reference to the major musical time periods from the Middle Ages to Modern times.

Videos

This collection of videos showcases the lives of some great composers through the eyes of a fictional child character. The book referenced underneath contains information and lesson plans to go with each video.

Bach's Fight for Freedom
Beethoven Lives Upstairs
Bizet's Dream
Liszt's Rhapsody
Rossini's Ghost
Strauss: The King of Three Quarter Time

The Composers' Specials; Teacher's Guide from the Devine Entertainment Video Series by Betsy Henderson

Visit this site to learn about Dennis Kobray, a musician/actor who personifies some of the great composers. His school performances are also available on DVD and VHS. Visit his website at http://www.meetthemusicians.us/

 Teacher's Notes:

 Teacher's Notes:

Inspired by Listening
is published in a perfect bound soft-cover edition.
The cover design is by: CRAFTMASTERS®
The layout is by Elizabeth Peterson.
The text is composed of
Times New Roman, Tempus Sans ITC, and Bradley Hand ITC.
This book has been printed by Thomson-Shore Inc.
on Joy White 60#, acid free paper.

Elizabeth M. Peterson received a B.S. in Elementary Education and a B.A. in Music at Gordon College in Wenham, Massachusetts, and earned an M.Ed. with a focus on "Arts and Learning" from Endicott College in Beverly, Massachusetts. Currently, she teaches general music and chorus to middle school students and is music consultant for the *Educational News Quarterly*. She also teaches private piano lessons, enjoys dance and living history reenactment. Mrs. Peterson lives in an 1840s farmhouse in New Hampshire with her husband Brad and son Zachary. At this writing she is expecting a baby in February.